The Needle Arts

T I M E - L I F E   B O O K S

Alexandria, Virginia

The Needle Arts

a social history of American needlework

A REBUS BOOK

CONTENTS

Needlework in the Home

Collecting by Design · A Respect for Fine Stitchery
An Eye for Comfort

144

NEEDLEWORK TECHNIQUES

166

CREDITS

168

INDEX

170

ACKNOWLEDGMENTS

175

The story of American needlework is essentially a woman's story. Nearly all of the stitchery presented in this volume—dating from the 1600s to the early 20th century—is the work of females, and it represents their most important contribution to the American decorative arts during this period. For the most part, it is distinguished by an artistry equal to that of other contemporary handcrafts, such as silversmithing and woodworking, that were traditionally in the male domain. A remarkable difference, however, is that stitchery was generally not the handiwork of professionals, but of school-age girls, or of women with homes and families demanding their full attention.

Undertaken along with many other household duties, needlework was an ever-present part of daily life, and it was advantageous to be good at it. Until the mid-19th century, in fact, a girl's skill with the needle symbolized her eligibility for marriage, and, once she was wed, it remained a measure of her success and value as a housewife. "Needle-work, in all its forms of use, elegance and ornament, has ever been the appropriate occupation of woman...," wrote Lydia Sigourney in her 1837 volume *Letters to Young Ladies*, "...it has been both their duty and their resource."

Those for whom needlework was primarily a "duty" often had to confine their labors to the plain sewing necessary for making bed and table linens, as well as the family's clothing. In 1889, one Lucy Larcom recalled thinking in her youth, "I suppose I have got to grow up and have a husband, and put all those little stitches into his coats and pantaloons. Oh, I never, never can do it!"

The kind of plain-sewn pieces that Lucy dreaded stitching were used and laundered until they fell apart; as a result, early examples are rare today. What has survived, as shown in this volume, is mostly fancywork: samplers, "best" quilts and coverlets, canvaswork table covers, crewelwork bed hangings, Berlin-work pictures, silk-embroidered tea cloths, and other pieces intended primarily for show.

The women who did such fancywork followed fads originating both in this country and in Europe, and the designs, colors, and stitches they employed were dictated by current fashions. In general, the makers were fortunate enough to have the time and money to spend on handiwork that would ensure a stylish decor. Yet, even beyond fashion, fancy needlework provided females with the important "resource" to which Lydia Sigourney referred: for most women who wielded a needle, it was one of the few available outlets for creativity, and the stitchery that has passed down through the generations constitutes an invaluable record of their artistry and skill. Today, fine needlework is prized not only for the ingenious approaches that the makers took in transforming fabric and thread into beautiful objects, but also for its craftsmanship. The hundreds or even thousands of stitches that went into each piece, and the innumerable hours of labor the finished works required, in themselves represent accomplishments that should not pass unnoticed.

Stitches in Time

*remarkable needlework from
the colonial period to the
Victorian era*

From the colonial era through much of the 1800s in America, almost all females sewed. For a well-to-do individual, "fancy sewing" provided an afternoon's pastime, but her skills in decorative needlework also presented proof that she was well trained in the social graces—and indeed a lady. For a woman in less comfortable circumstances, practical "plain" work was an endless necessity; she made and mended her family's clothing, hemmed and marked the household linens, and knitted mittens and socks.

The styles and techniques of both decorative embroidery and plainwork hold an important place in the history of American needle arts. Some, like lacework, memorial embroidery, and Victorian Berlin work, were passing fashions, while others, such as knitting, remained mainstays throughout the years. Together, they offer a compelling insight into the nature of women's lives during America's first three centuries.

A detail from a circa 1750 canvaswork picture (page 24) demonstrates the fine workmanship that was characteristic of tent stitch.

American Samplers

Before the 19th century, sewing instruction was the only education that many females received. Lessons began in childhood, and the standard teaching tool was the sampler: a piece of cloth (usually linen) on which needlework techniques were practiced. The sampler tradition was brought to this country by settlers in the 17th century. Although embroidery books were then being printed in Europe, they were rare, and samplers provided a more accessible means of recording stitches.

The earliest American samplers were very narrow in shape, measuring up to thirty inches long and eight inches wide. Stylized designs in silk or linen thread were stitched across the fabric background in formal rows; the same motifs and stitches could then be easily copied on a bed sheet or tablecloth. Finely worked, such samplers typically included the decorative eyelet, arrowhead, Montenegrin, and spider web stitches, as well as the versatile cross-stitch.

Little thought was given to the design of such fancywork pieces, since they were not meant for display but were instead kept rolled up in a sewing basket. Used throughout a woman's life, they could be pulled out and consulted when necessary, and perhaps further embellished when new stitches were learned. During the

Continued

Mary Holingworth's circa 1665 fancywork sampler, right, is one of the earliest known pieces made in America. It measures 25 inches long and only 7½ inches wide.

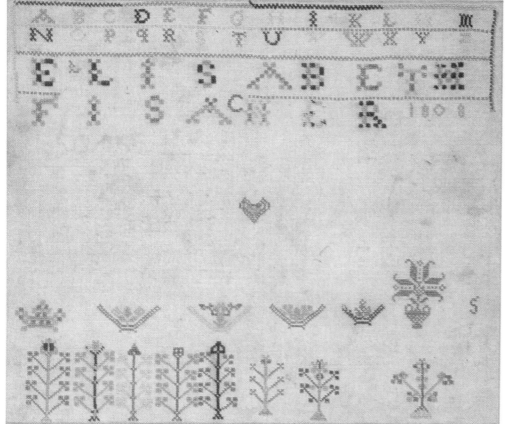

Most young girls worked on "marking samplers" in order to learn useful stitches. The circa 1815 piece above was made by Betsy Crosman, who was raised by the Shakers. Elisabeth Fisher, an Amish girl, used traditional Pennsylvania-German motifs on her 1808 sampler, left.

The 1752 Philadelphia lacework piece above was done entirely in cutwork by Rebekah Jones. Frances Paschal of Delaware used two lacework techniques in her 1788 sampler, right. The corner circles and her name are done in cutwork, while the delicate leaves and flower petals show off her skills at drawnwork.

1700s, samplers became increasingly shorter—and more manageable for young fingers—until by the end of the century they were small rectangles or squares. Within the new format, needleworkers began to combine lettering with decorative borders and motifs, creating artistic compositions designed to be displayed like pictures.

While fancywork samplers continued to be made, more practical types were also done in the 18th century. The most common were "marking samplers," comprising numerals and the letters of the alphabet sewn in cross-stitch. Working on such a sampler allowed a young girl to learn her numbers and letters, and even more important, it enabled her to mark linens and clothing. This was a necessary chore at a time when a family

might have as many as fifteen children in it.

Equally useful for teaching an important skill were darning samplers, which also had become popular by the middle of the 1700s. In these samplers, holes were made in a piece of fabric and then "repaired"; the finished works showed off the needleworker's prowess at imitating the variety of fabric weaves that she would no doubt encounter during a lifetime of mending.

Fashionable 18th-century ladies with time at their disposal might try their hand at lacework, which was used to imitate expensive imported trimmings. Thus samplers were also made with lacy designs done in cutwork, a technique in which shapes were cut out of a piece of fine cotton or linen and then filled in with rows and webs of buttonhole stitches. Another method

Continued

American women began making darning samplers in the 1700s and continued the practice over the course of the next century; the cotton-on-linen piece at left dates to 1873. Its fine workmanship demonstrates how the weaves of twills and other fabrics could be imitated with darning. Colored threads permitted the needleworker to see that her stitches were perfectly aligned.

Ann Wheeley worked the words, flower motifs, and heart-decorated bands on the linen sampler at right entirely in cross-stitch. Schoolgirl samplers like Ann's piece, done in 1832 when she was eleven, frequently incorporated verses; God, death, and one's reward in heaven were popular subjects.

was drawn-thread work, also known as Dresden work, which involved removing several warp or weft threads from the fabric weave and pulling the remaining threads together with embroidery stitches to form delicate patterns.

Throughout most of the 1700s, decorative and practical needlework were taught at home, but by the end of the century it was possible for more and more children to learn the needle arts in the private schools that were beginning to proliferate. The very young might attend a "dame's school," which was usually run by a sin-

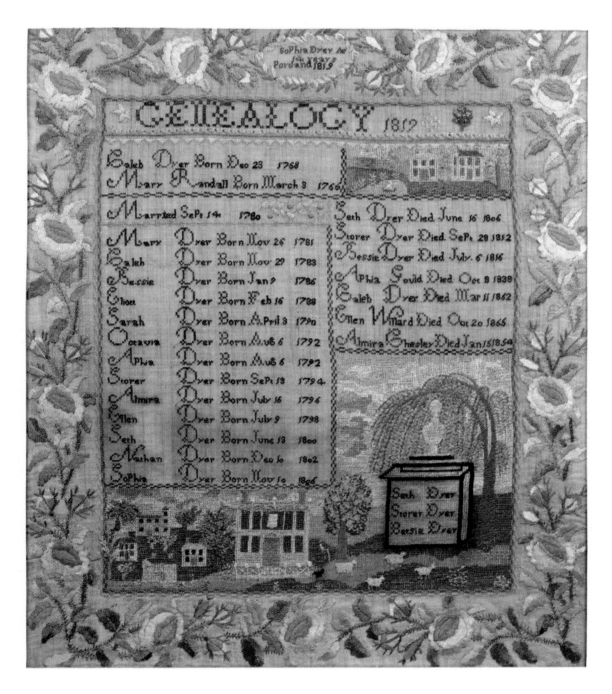

Typical of genealogical samplers, the 1819 silk-on-linen piece at left, by Sophia Dyer, was stitched with the needleworker's family record and a memorial scene. Such embroideries were ongoing projects, and the dates of marriages and deaths were often added in many years after the sampler was begun.

gle woman or widow in her home. Here, both boys and girls learned to sew by working a cross-stitch alphabet sampler, and perhaps studied the rudiments of reading.

For many girls, schooling ended at the dame's school. With their knowledge of basic sewing, females could be more useful at home, especially if finances were limited. When family circumstances demanded, some girls were indentured as housekeepers or seamstresses in wealthy households in return for room and board. The hope was that at the end of her service, a young wom-

Continued

The 1799 sampler above represents the family record of Leah Galligher and Rachel Armstrong, twin sisters who ran a school in Pennsylvania.

an would have the housewifely skills needed to attract a husband despite her lack of dowry.

If her family was affluent, however, a girl was likely to be sent to a needlework school or to a private young ladies' academy. Here she might stay for a few quarters or for several years (pupils were generally in their teens, but might be as young as ten or as old as thirty). While most academies offered subjects such as French and history, they were essentially finishing schools, and emphasis was placed on dancing, draw-

ing, deportment, and, of course, needlework.

Having already worked an alphabet sampler as a young girl, the academy student was taught to make a fancier type of needlework piece, if she had the talent. These schoolgirl samplers continued to include neat rows of cross-stitched letters, but the compositions, incorporating biblical verses, sentimental poetry, and pictorial borders, were considerably more involved than those of plain alphabet samplers. Many pieces included a record of births, deaths, and mar-

See youth and beauty bloom one transient hour
But age leaves not one flatering trace behind
But there is one charm over which time has no Power
The beauty of a cultivated mind

Haste then dear youth and make this charm thine own
See meek religion Points You out the way
Give her thy hand and She will lead thee on
Where virtue blossms in eternal day

Wrought by Catharine Mary Wheeler in the 13 year of her age Jane Keys Instructress of Brunswick School 1825

riages in the needleworker's family; such gene-alogical samplers were one of the most popular sampler forms in America, and are thought to have originated in this country.

The designs of schoolgirl samplers, common-ly stitched in linen or silk thread on a linen or linsey-woolsey ground, were usually devised by the teacher rather than by the student, and in-cluded original creations as well as adaptations of English prototypes. Traditional folk motifs were often worked into the compositions, as were "portraits" of family homes or local landmarks. Because specific stitching styles and imagery became popular in certain parts of the country, samplers from a particular town or school tend-ed to look alike. The stitches varied with the type of picture, but typically included satin, split, Gobelin, and chain stitches, French knots, and couching. Such fancywork would not be useful in plain sewing, but it did show off a girl's ability with a needle. The object of her labors, after all, was to ensure a suitable marriage.

The designs of the house and stepped lawn on the sampler above are typical of pieces from the Delaware River Valley. The two shepherd-esses and the sheep were done in silk-embroidered appliqué.

The long, diagonal crinkled-silk stitches used to fill in the background of the sampler above are characteristic of pieces made at Sarah Stivour's school in Salem, Massachusetts. The crinkling, which occurred when embroidery thread was unraveled, was favored for its especially shiny effect.

Samplers done on a colored ground, like the piece above, by Beulah Purinton of Massachusetts, are rare.

Beulah worked her design in French knots and satin, whip, and eyelet stitches, using crinkled silk.

As is common, the script alphabet is missing the letters I and U.

PRACTICAL POCKETS

Anyone who remembers the nursery rhyme in which "Lucy Locket lost her pocket" may also recall wondering how she did it. In fact, in Lucy's day, misplacing a pocket was not at all improbable, for, until the 1840s, pockets were not sewn into clothing but were worn separately. A woman would tie her pockets (generally made in pairs) by a string around her waist, placing them under her skirt and over her petticoat. Sometimes measuring as long as fifteen inches, generously sized pockets like the antique pieces at right might be used to hold sewing or knitting projects; slits in the side seams of the wearer's skirt provided access to the contents.

Although the pockets were not usually visible, they could be surprisingly decorative, and might be elaborately embroidered. Such fancywork pockets were often made by young ladies to be part of their trousseaux, or were stitched as gifts. Making pockets was also an ideal project for a child learning to sew. At her mother's knee a little girl could stitch her first patchwork, seams, and bindings, ending up with her own colorful carryalls.

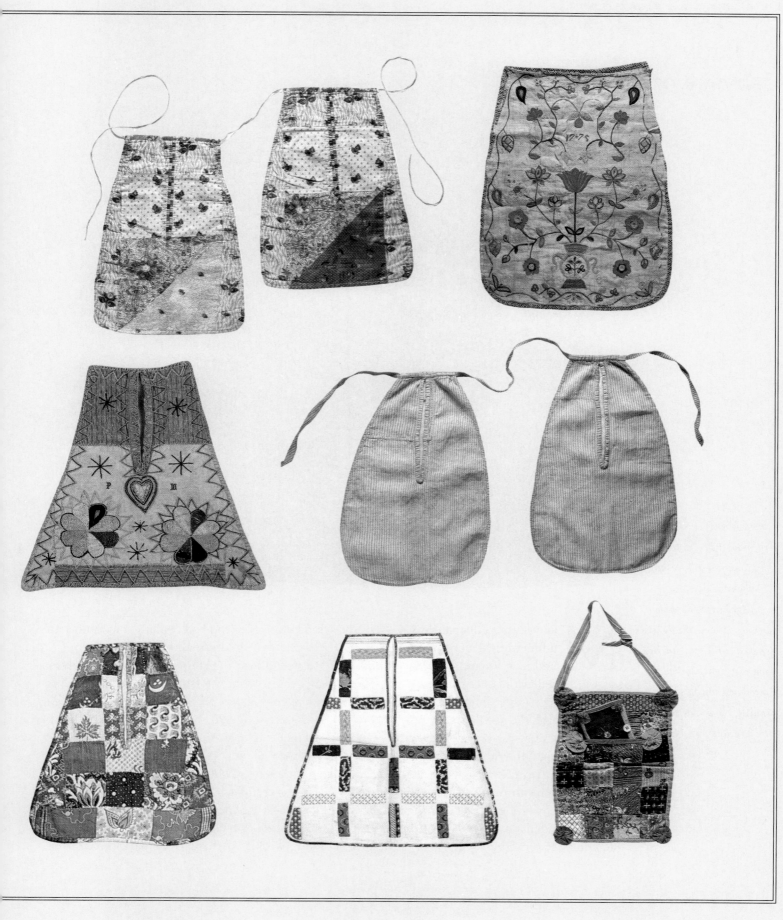

Early Canvaswork

Canvaswork pictures made in the mid-18th century were apt to show well-dressed ladies and gentlemen engaged in fashionable pastimes. Among the figures depicted in the tent-stitched piece at right, worked in wool and silk on a linen canvas, is a couple seated at a gaming table.

Magnificent craftsmanship was greatly admired by Americans in the 1700s, and it is not surprising that much of the finest needlework ever stitched in this country dates from that century. Among the most distinctive of all the needle arts fashionable at the time was canvaswork—now known as needlepoint—a type of embroidery worked on an open-weave canvas mesh usually made of linen or hemp. Done throughout the colonies, most early canvaswork pieces were the handiwork of academy students and women of means, since such complex embroidery was out of the ques-

tion for anyone who had cooking, mending, and a houseful of children to attend to.

Stitched over the entire surface of the canvas, early canvaswork was generally done in silk floss or crewel—a two-ply, loosely twisted worsted wool yarn—in tent, queen, and Irish stitches. The tent stitch was simple but tedious to execute because each stitch covered only one thread of the canvas mesh, which was typically very finely woven—as tight as fifty-two threads per inch. (The finest needlepoint canvas used today has only twenty-four threads per inch.) Such painstaking work is particularly remarkable, consid-

ering the poor lighting conditions of the time.

Because the tight, tiny tent stitches produced finer detail than any other canvaswork stitch, they were favored for the intricate scenic and floral pictures popular in the 18th century. The effects that could be achieved in a tent-stitched picture were so rich, in fact, that such canvaswork was thought to resemble European tapestries, and the technique was sometimes called tapestrywork. Tent-stitched compositions were generally made by advanced students at the few ladies' academies that existed in the mid-1700s. Requiring a year or more to execute, the projects were probably completed as graduation pieces and taken home to be framed and displayed.

Among the most famous tent-stitched scenes are those referred to as the Fishing Lady pictures (overleaf). Made in Boston at mid-century, about sixty of these pieces are now known to exist. Although they differ in size and composition, the works share common pictorial elements. They are usually pastoral scenes; some feature a beautifully dressed lady angler—fishing was a popular pastime for courting couples in the 18th century—others a reclining shepherdess. The pieces are thought to have been

Continued

The fanciful canvaswork picture above was done by Mary Whitehead around 1750. Often, no attempt was made to achieve realistic perspective in such tent-stitched designs; flowers could be the size of people, and birds the size of buildings.

Nearly four feet wide, the Fishing Lady pictures above were made as "chimney pieces," to hang over the fireplace. Very similar in design, the compositions were worked by two different young ladies from Cape Cod, who are thought to have studied in Boston with the needlework teacher Susannah Condy.

Many Boston pictures done in canvaswork were similar to the Fishing Lady designs but lacked the lovely female angler. The piece stitched by Hannah Carter around 1750, top, features a lady holding a fan, and the circa 1775 picture by Mary Woodhull, bottom, was designed as a harvest scene.

The circa 1740 Boston canvaswork chair seat above was done in tent stitch. The difficult queen stitch was used for the silk-embroidered pocketbook at top right, while the piece at bottom right displays an Irish-stitched flame pattern.

worked by students of Mrs. Susannah Condy, a needlework teacher and designer in Boston. Mrs. Condy evidently adapted her designs from English and French prints, often embellishing them with flowers, foliage, and birds that were indigenous to America.

Decorative pictures such as the Fishing Lady scenes, as well as other pieces done in canvaswork, such as fire screens, table covers, and chair seats, were welcome additions to the colonial home. These luxurious furnishings—a clear reflection of a family's status in the community—were coveted and proudly shown off.

Indeed, among a woman's most important contributions to a well-to-do household was fine

stitchery. While her skill with the needle was appreciated by family members, the personal possessions, clothing, and home furnishings she turned out by hand were also expected to be admired by everyone else who saw them. This was especially true of canvaswork; the stitchery required expensive wool and silk yarns, clearly demonstrating that the needleworker enjoyed the luxuries of both time and money.

Dutiful wives and daughters spent hours stitching canvaswork pieces that were serviceable as well as beautiful. Imported canvases pre-drawn with the patterns for such articles could be purchased from "fancy shops," but they were extremely costly. A woman might also go to a

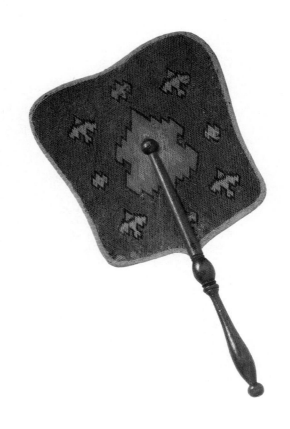

local needlework professional to have a canvas prepared, or she could take lessons and learn to draw designs in ink on canvas herself.

Chair seats were generally worked in Irish stitch, which was relatively quick to do because each stitch covered three or four threads of canvas. Worked into a colorful flame-shaped pattern, zigzags, or diamonds in diamonds, Irish stitch was also popular for making small pocketbooks. If a woman was extremely ambitious, however, she would craft a pocketbook in queen stitch—the most intricate and difficult of all canvaswork stitches. Such beautifully stitched pocketbooks were frequently made as gifts for loved ones and were customarily embellished with the name of

the owner and perhaps the date the piece was completed. Men carried pocketbooks in their coat pockets to protect important papers and currency, while women customarily used theirs for storing jewelry or trinkets.

Canvaswork fire screens were also put to good use at a time when staying warm in the winter meant sitting close to the hearth. Usually square or rectangular, large screens were mounted in wood-backed frames; these were attached to an adjustable pole stand that was set in front of the fire. Small screens, by contrast, were designed to be hand-held. The purpose of both types was to protect the face from heat and glare while the rest of one's body stayed warm.

The richly colored fire screen panel above left, made by Tanneke Pears, was done in Irish stitch and includes a wry verse at the bottom. The hand-held fire screen above right, also in Irish stitch, shows similar motifs; both pieces date to the 1700s.

PRUDENCE PUNDERSON

Prudence Punderson's c. 1775 embroidery above is housed in the Connecticut Historical Society along with many of the furnishings depicted.

Few American needlework pictures of the 18th century reveal as much about the women who made them as those of Prudence Punderson. Born in Preston, Connecticut, in 1758, Punderson studied embroidery as a girl and became a true artist with her needle; her work is notable both for its quality and for the many delightful details she borrowed from the world around her.

Prudence Punderson's best-known embroidery, a depiction of life's passing entitled "The First, Second, and Last Scene of Mortality," was worked when she was about sixteen. The piece is remarkable for its candid

glimpse of her family's parlor, a stylish room furnished with Chippendale chairs, a patterned carpet, and a framed needlework picture. The subject for "life's passing" is Punderson herself, portrayed as an infant with her nanny, as a young and well-dressed woman—at work on a piece of embroidery—and, finally, nailed into a coffin marked with her initials. (The gilded mirror hanging behind the coffin is shrouded in linen, following a mourning custom of the day.) It turned out that Punderson's own life was, in fact, quite brief, ending when she was only twenty-six years old.

Less poignant than her parlor scene, yet equally original, is a set of individual portraits depicting the twelve Apostles, stitched by Punderson between 1776 and 1780. The spiritual subjects are definitely of this world; the barefoot Saint Peter, for instance, wears an American tricorn hat and is seated in a Queen Anne chair, while Saint Simon clutches a saw. Punderson's choice of a religious theme for her series of portraits was not unusual for the 18th century, but the freshness and imagination she brought to her remarkable needlework designs were very much her own.

The four needlework portraits above are from Prudence Punderson's series of the twelve Apostles. Clockwise from top left, they include Saint Peter, Judas Iscariot, Saint Simon the Zealot, and Saint John the Evangelist. Like all of Punderson's known needlework pictures, they were worked in silk on a silk-satin background.

Silkwork Pictures

While the trees of the circa 1820 piece above were stitched in silk, the rest of the picture was done in watercolor; the two mediums were often combined in early-19th-century schoolgirl pieces.

Embroidered pictures worked in silk on a silk-satin ground first became fashionable in this country in the mid-1700s. Because silk had to be imported from Europe at that time, the early pieces were extremely costly to undertake. After the Revolution was over, however, America began trading directly with China, and the price of the materials dropped. By around 1800, a fad for silkwork caught on in England, and the technique immediately became extremely popular among American academy students, remaining so through the 1820s.

While the earlier silkwork pictures were more closely related to samplers, the 19th-century pieces were conceived almost as silk paintings, and their makers—who might labor on a piece during the course of several school terms—considered themselves to be true artists.

Ye stubborn oaks, and stately pines, Ye birds, his praise must be your theme, Ye flow'ry plains, proclaim his skill;
Bend your high branches and adore. Who form'd to song your tuneful voice. Ye vallies, sink before his eyes
Praise God, ye beasts in different str- While the dumb fish that cuts the stre- And let his praise from every hill,ces.
The lamb must bleat the oxen roar. In his protecting care rejoice. Rise tune ful to the neighb'ring ski-

MARY REES 1827   E. Robinson Teacher

The scenes academy pupils chose to stitch in the 1800s also differed in that they reflected the changes beginning to take place in female education. Along with needlework and other "accomplishments," genteel young ladies were now expected to improve their minds. They read novels, studied religion and literature, and analyzed the classical civilizations whose democratic ideals were the models for America's new repub-

lic. Often working from English print sources, girls stitched biblical and literary scenes to show off their knowledge. Characters in their pictures might be dressed in classical garb, and the compositions were apt to include marble temples and perhaps a few verses of lofty poetry expressing the popular themes of love, heroism, and virtue.

These themes and imagery found their full

Continued

Mary Rees stitched the bucolic pastoral scene above on linen, using silk for all of the embroidery except for the sheep's coats, which were done in wool. Her teacher's name also appears.

Beautifully worked in silk, the memorial embroideries above and at right show scrupulous attention to detail; even the stone in the plinths was stitched to resemble veined marble. The Burgess piece also records detailed tomb inscriptions for the needleworker's mother and two brothers.

This device was begun by Isabella Caldwell Dana who died ere it was finished
"Early bright transient, chaste, as morning dew,
She sparkled was exhal'd and went to Heav'n"

flowering in the vogue for memorial embroideries, which lasted from the late 18th century until the 1830s. Typically featuring elaborate plinths and tombstones, weeping willows, and tearful mourners, these romanticized compositions were all too often stitched by girls following the loss of family members. Many needlework pieces were also made to commemorate George Washington, whose death in 1799 had

an enormous emotional impact on the nation.

As somber as their subject matter was, however, memorial pictures were considered to be stylish home furnishings rather than the morbid mementos they seem today. Worked in silk, chenille, and sparkling metallic threads, the pictures were proudly displayed, appealing as much to the current taste for the classical and antique as to the fashion for sentimentality.

Memorials were often true expressions of grief. Fifteen-year-old Isabella Dana began the picture at left around 1804, in memory of her father, Josiah. After Isabella died in 1805 her bereaved sister, Sarah, continued the piece. Before the work was finished, however, it was necessary to add the name of her mother, who died two months after Isabella.

FANCYWORK FROM "GODEY'S"

Basket decorated with crystal beads

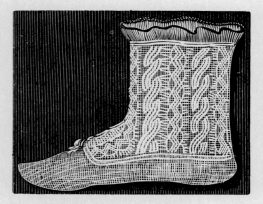

Knitted baby's shoe and sock

Hanging pincushion and needlebook

Beginning in the 1830s, innumerable fads for decorative embroidery developed in America and were pursued with widespread enthusiasm by the many middle-class ladies who now had leisure time on their hands. In large part, the interest in needlework novelties was kindled by a wholly new phenomenon: women's magazines. There were several such publications, including *Graham's* and *Peterson's,* but the most popular was *Godey's Lady's Book,* which was founded in 1830 by Louis A. Godey, and edited from 1837 to 1877 by Sarah Josepha Hale—one of America's first female editors.

Establishing a format that is still followed by many women's magazines today, *Godey's* was a compendium of contemporary fiction and articles on health, gardening, women's education, child rearing, and fashion. Each issue also included instructions for fancywork crafts, accompanied by engraved illustrations like those at right. Patterns for Berlin work appeared, as well as many other suggestions for projects involving popular techniques such as beadwork, knitting, crocheting, and punched-paper work.

Punched-paper watch pocket

Slipper watch stand

Beaded napkin ring

Berlin-work button case

Knitted reticule

Punched-paper sewing basket

Beaded butterfly penwipe

Knitted baby's glove

Crocheted knitting bag

Victorian Berlin Work

As public schools became more prevalent in the 1830s, the emphasis in women's education shifted from "accomplishments" to the basics of reading, writing, and arithmetic. Some girls still learned sewing in school, but concentrated on plainwork rather than fancywork. Other girls grew up without ever working a sampler at all. Yet, while females were no longer concerned with mastering intricate embroidery, they remained interested in needlework as a pleasurable pastime. That interest was reflected by the rage for a type of canvaswork called Berlin-wool work, or simply Berlin work, by far the most popular type of stitchery done between the 1830s and 1870s.

Berlin work was easier to do than earlier canvaswork because it was stitched with the help of patterns (first printed in Berlin, Germany) that eliminated any need for conceiving a design, determining shading, or choosing colors. Moreover, most such work was done with German merino wool yarns, known as Berlin wool. Softer and thicker than the crewel yarns used for early canvaswork, Berlin wool was worked on a relatively open-mesh canvas—about twenty-four threads to the inch—which made projects move along quickly. Since entire Berlin-work designs were often done with a single type of stitch (usually tent, cross, or Irish) virtually any woman could become adept at the craft. Best of all, however, Berlin work was versatile. It could be, and was, used for the wide range of projects—including carpet slippers, sentimental pictures, pincushions, ottomans, lambrequins, and bellpulls—favored during the Victorian period.

Berlin-work patterns could be used with a variety of materials. The circa 1845 still-life design, top, was stitched in wool and silk on a linen background. The picture at bottom, which dates to around 1840, is worked in silk on silk mesh.

*Victorian lambrequins, or valances, were used across the tops of windows and interior doorways, and
also as shelf trims. The paisley and leaf Berlin-work design, top, was done in tent stitch, the flame
design, center, in Irish stitch, and the abstract floral design, bottom, in cross-stitch.*

Entitled "Family Happiness," the picture above was one of many popular mid-19th-century Berlin-work designs that featured sentimental scenes of family life.

German publishers catered to American tastes by devising Berlin-work patterns that pictured well-loved national heroes such as Ben Franklin, who is depicted in the mid-19th-century piece above.

The lively picture above, stitched by Phebe Kriebel in 1857, is similar to several others known to have been made in Pennsylvania. Far more original in character than most Berlin-work designs, Phebe's piece nevertheless displays many of the standard motifs, such as the bunches of pink roses and the reclining spaniels, favored in the Victorian age.

By the mid-1870s, Berlin work was no longer a widespread fad, but women continued to stitch designs
on canvas. Worked between 1883 and 1886, the picture above is a sampler of sorts, combining
traditional Berlin-work designs—such as the calla lilies, horse's head, and cat—with familiar,
everyday images, like the cigar, house, and little red chair.

42

BERLIN-WORK PATTERNS

Early in the 19th century, German printers in Berlin devised a means of mapping out canvas-work designs on a type of graph, or "point," paper. On black-and-white patterns, the squares of the graph were marked with tiny symbols indicating what shade of wool was to be used. Colored patterns—at first hand-painted, and eventually printed—were also available. The needleworker followed the patterns simply by counting squares on the graph and stitching in the appropriate colors on the canvas. It was even easier to use patterns for punched-paper work—a Berlin-work variation that appeared in the 1870s—as these were printed right onto the perforated cards that were to be stitched.

Imported Berlin-work patterns were used in America to a limited extent until the 1840s, when women's periodicals began including reproductions of the patterns and suggestions for copying them; patterns were also available in "fancy shops." Publishers in Vienna and Paris soon followed Germany's lead in devising designs, and thousands were produced. They ranged from geometric and floral patterns—used for such furnishings and accessories as footstools, sofa pillows, pincushions, and tea cozies—to scenes that could be framed and displayed as pictorial "art." Over time, the designs became increasingly sentimental and ornate in response to Victorian tastes.

Plushwork

The King Charles spaniel, the particular breed owned by Queen Victoria, became a popular subject in 19th-century needlework. In the picture above, the dog's coat, face, and paws were executed in plushwork, a variation on the Berlin-work technique.

For the most part, Victorian house interiors leaned toward decorative excess. In an era when no surface was left uncovered, middle-class women were always on the lookout for projects that would keep their hands busy and add that extra exotic, colorful, or sentimental touch to their rooms. If nothing else, the abundance of household embellishments that women managed to turn out during the Victorian period represented the virtues of industriousness and a tireless devotion to feathering the family nest.

As the taste for novelty increased, several variations on Berlin work developed that could be made using the same patterns. Among these was plushwork, which was characterized by raised stitches (like those on hooked rugs) that formed a napped surface. Left untrimmed, the stitches created a long, loopy effect; cropped close, they yielded a soft, fuzzy surface. If the needleworker desired, she could appliqué a plushwork design to a solid-colored fabric; this eliminated the laborious task of filling in the background of a piece with stitching.

The maker of the table cover above stitched the plushwork hunting scene and corner designs directly onto a wool background. The floral border is done in Berlin work.

Punched Paper

Stitching punched-paper designs for bookmarks was especially fast and easy, since the background area was almost never filled in. Ribbon bookmarks like the 19th-century pieces at right were considered appropriate gifts for children to make for their teachers, family, and friends.

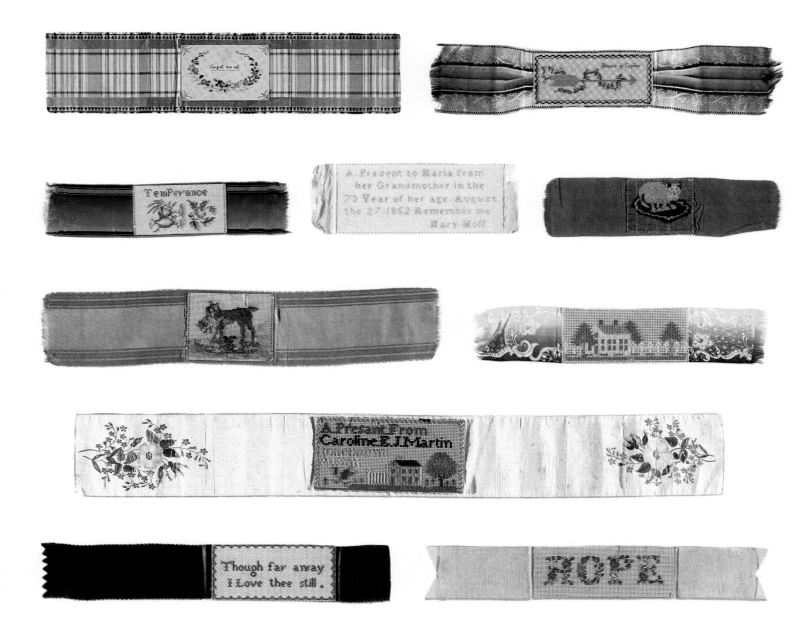

Beginning in the 1840s, the patterns used for Berlin work were also adapted for a new craft in which stitches were worked through a stiff paper or cardboard backing punched with evenly spaced holes. Punched-paper needlework, favored for small pictures and accessories, became a fad primarily because the materials were so inexpensive. For only a few pennies, it was possible for a needleworker to stitch small designs like those sewn onto the ribbon bookmarks shown here. Often incorporating an inspirational motto, such pieces were frequently stitched as gifts or mementos.

By the 1870s, the fashion for punched paper had also extended to larger pictures (overleaf). The needleworker could either draw her own design on a perforated background sheet, or buy one that was already printed; long horizontal or diagonal stitches were sometimes used for these quick-to-execute projects.

Most punched-paper designs were stitched with fine wool, but silk, metallic threads, and beads might be added, as on the bookmarks above.

These late-19th-century punched-paper pictures show similar houses, with imaginative variations on the theme. Bits of lace and fabric were worked into the piece at top, while the design at bottom is embellished with lithographed paper cutouts.

Many of the most popular punched-paper patterns sold in the late 19th century featured homely sayings or blessings like those stitched into the pictures at left. Often done in variegated wools, such pieces were customarily framed and hung over doorways.

Beadwork Accessories

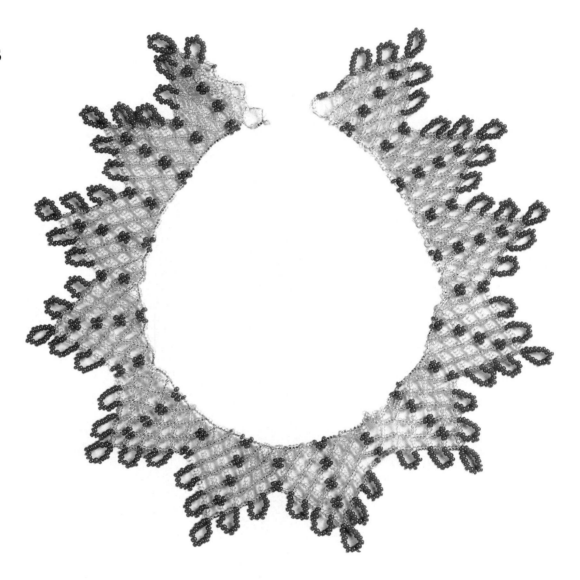

By threading tiny glass beads, Victorian women produced elaborate pieces like the collar above. Directions for such projects often appeared in ladies' magazines of the period.

In the early years of the 19th century, the art of beadwork—making sewn or knitted articles decorated with beads—was taught at some girls' schools, and by the 1830s, the craft had come into vogue among middle-class women. In some respects, its popularity was linked to that of Berlin work, since the color-coded grids of Berlin patterns could easily be adapted to pieces worked with tiny glass or steel beads.

Because beadwork was slow going, and the finished articles relatively heavy, most projects were quite small. Tiny handbags were partic-

ularly popular. To make one, a woman might stitch beads onto a fabric ground, work beads into knitting, or weave thread and beads together on a small loom; metal closures or frames with delicate chain handles could be purchased, but homemade designs for drawstring bags were also common.

Other accessories, such as collars, required threading the beads. Simple threading produced tassels and fringe; more complex techniques yielded weblike patterns that could be applied over fabric, as well as the intricate openwork favored for jewelry and hair ornaments.

The beadwork bags above show some of the many variations that were possible in this time-consuming craft. The pictorial designs were adapted from Berlin-work patterns, while the small handbag at bottom center was made by incorporating beads into silk knitting. The mesh covering the black silk bag at bottom right is worked with beads and pumpkin seeds.

PURLS OF WISDOM

While it was not essential for the woman in Victorian America to knit in order to keep her family in warm clothing—as it had been for her colonial counterpart—the Puritan work ethic continued to dictate that her hands be busy during her waking hours. Lest she forget this, ladies' magazines and books of the period bombarded her with the message that, in order to be a good wife, she had to be forever making things to beautify her home. The 1894 edition of *Dainty Work for Pleasure and Profit,* for example, made it clear that a diligent homemaker should use her "nimble fingers" to create "accessories in the shape of mantel drapes, screens, wall-pockets, toilet sets, dainty table linen, cushions, photograph holders, and all the numberless odds and ends that go to make up the pretty home . . . ."

There were other, cautionary lessons to be heeded as well. An 1887 book entitled *Knitting and Crochet: A Guide to the Use of the Needle and the Hook* counseled knitters that, when young, their skill with the needles might be "a defense against weariness," but that by the time they reached middle age, "that terrible period to women, when they have lost the charm of youth, without acquiring the veneration due to age," knitting would be a way to "lighten their monotonous hours . . . ."

Women's publications further suggested that homemakers knit while engaged in other activities, such as reading or nursing a baby. In 1848, *A Winter Gift for Ladies* proposed that women knit "when passing a morning visit, or after dinner at a dinner party, or while sipping coffee, or taking ices at the public gardens . . . ."

And although such needlework treatises also proclaimed knitting to be "the friend of the aged and blind," and a skill that even the "most stupid" could practice, the instructions they offered were generally so complicated as to baffle the most astute knitter. The *Ladies' Guide to Needlework,* published in 1877, acknowledged this by commenting that if two different women used the same yarn and the same needles to make a tidy, "one would produce a square hardly large enough to cover a pincushion, while the work of the other could be used for a bed-spread."

Knitting

Knitting is one of the earliest, most practical, and longest-lasting of all the needle arts in America. During the colonial period, children were taught to knit by the time they were six years old. Even though the colonies imported knitted goods from England, there was a never-ending need for more warm mittens and caps in the winter, and stockings all year round. (Colonial men traditionally wore white stockings, but females wore colorful versions under their long skirts.)

Some colonial women—and men too—earned an income by knitting professionally. More often, however, wives and daughters produced the knitted goods used by their families. Warm clothing was knitted from wool, while more personal articles such as decorative little handbags —usually the province of delicate ladies—were traditionally worked in silk.

Fortunately, knitting was not the most arduous of chores. It was easily picked up and put down, and could be carried from one place to another. Since knitting left the mind free while keeping the hands busy, women often worked on their projects during visits with their friends over tea, or while listening to their children recite school lessons at home.

Knitting remained popular among the well-to-do until the Civil War, for making such articles as lace, shawls, and throws. But by the turn of the century, the taste for such pieces had faded, and knitting, too, fell from fashion, becoming, for the time being, a pastime mainly of the elderly.

Worked on tiny needles, the small silk handbags above were all knitted by Mary Wright Alsop of Middletown, Connecticut, in the early 19th century.

The mittens and gloves at right date from the mid-19th century to about 1920. Those in the top row were all made in New England. The heavy shag-knitted pieces in the middle row also come from New England and are sometimes referred to as sleigh gloves. The striped mittens in the bottom row were knitted by members of an Amish community in Indiana.

Hand-knitted woolen stockings were worn by men and women in this country until the early 1900s, and by children until the 1930s. The children's stockings in the top row were made in New England in the late 1800s. The socks in the bottom row were knitted by Amish women in the late 19th century. Bright colors were not incorporated into Amish designs until after 1860, but even then, decorative patterns were used only at the stocking tops, where they were hidden by clothing.

The Well-Dressed Bed

traditional quilts, spreads, blankets, and hangings stitched in America

In the colonial period, when a single room served numerous purposes, the master bed—often the most expensive piece of furniture in a household—was customarily placed in the parlor. There it served as a showpiece, perhaps dressed with a handsome yarn-sewn bed rug, or with a set of crewel-embroidered bed "furniture" that might include an intricately stitched coverlet and several hangings.

By the mid-1700s, the notion of privacy, and of separate rooms for sleeping, had become more widespread, and the bed was no longer such a prominent furnishing. Effort and time, however, were still devoted to stitching beautiful bedcovers—although the more elaborate of these were often put away in dower chests. Included among the remarkable range of pieces produced over the years are embroidered woolen blankets, cotton coverlets, whitework spreads, and of course, the familiar quilts that have become hallmarks of American needlework.

Appliquéd animals, including a pair of ostriches, can be seen in a detail of a finely stitched 19th-century quilt top (page 83).

Woolen Bed Rugs

The bed rug above, dated 1724, is one of the oldest known to exist. It was probably made by Catherine Thorn of Ipswich, Massachusetts, as a wedding gift for her sister Mary.

Among the most remarkable types of coverlets crafted in early America are the heavy woolen rugs that were generally used as warm top covers over layers of bedclothes. Produced primarily between the early 1700s and early 1800s, these bed rugs were made by sewing multi-ply woolen yarn through a woven fabric background of linen or wool. Some were done in flat stitches, but the majority were worked with running loops, which were often left uncut to create a plush pile surface; they might, however, also be trimmed.

While plain bed rugs are mentioned in early records, most of those that survive today (fewer than fifty) display bold patterns. These elaborate needlework pieces were the pride of their makers and were thus carefully preserved and passed down through many generations.

Making a bed rug was indeed an ambitious undertaking, as the rugs were not created from

scraps, but were instead carefully planned, incorporating materials that were specially prepared at home for the project. Of the hand-mixed dyes, dark blue was the most common color, since the indigo used to make it was fairly easy to obtain, and was colorfast. Brown and natural shades were also prevalent; yarns in greens and reds, which were hard colors to produce, were generally used sparingly.

Although none of the surviving bed rugs are identical, their patterns often reveal a striking similarity. The dramatic floral designs, including the popular tree of life motif, that characterize many of the rugs were almost certainly influenced by the embroidered and printed patterns found on English bed coverlets of the period. Some bed rug designs also appear to have been inspired by crewelwork bed hangings, and still others by the block-printed papers used to line English document boxes.

Twenty-year-old Deborah Loomis stitched the bed rug above around 1772. The coverlet features a tree of life design, popular at the time, and an unusual sky-blue background.

Hannah Johnson of Bozrah, Connecticut, stitched the bed rug above in 1796, when she was an unmarried

lady of twenty-six. Such pieces were often made to mark special occasions, and Hannah may have

created this rug in anticipation of her wedding.

After a lifetime of sewing, seventy-one-year-old Rachel Packard from Jericho, Vermont, was certainly
an experienced needlewoman when she stitched the rug above, completed in 1805. The bold
floral motifs resemble those found in 18th-century canvaswork.

By inscribing her name boldly over the stylized vase of flowers on the rug above, Mary Comstock of Shelburne, Vermont, showed she was proud of the piece, which she finished at age sixty-six.

The bed rug above, stitched by Dorothy Seabury of Stowe, Vermont, was worked primarily in browns,

which were relatively easy colors to produce with homemade dyes.

Crewelwork Bed Furniture

In the 17th and 18th centuries, beds in every colonial household of sufficient means were dressed for warmth and privacy with sets of "bed furniture," which might include a coverlet, a headcloth, three or four valances (depending on whether the bed was against the wall), side curtains, a tester cloth (canopy), and bases, attached to the bed rail.

Embroidered bed furniture was probably first made in this country in the 1700s. The various pieces were usually worked on linen or linen-blend backgrounds and stitched with crewel, a loosely twisted, two-ply woolen yarn. While the linen and the yarn were produced domestically, they were also imported from England, where crewelwork developed in the 1500s.

Many of the designs found in American crewelwork—which was used for draperies, upholstery, and clothing as well—also came from abroad, and were copied from pattern books brought to this country by settlers. Even designs originated by American needlework teachers or by the embroiderer herself were influenced by the English penchant for elaborate nature scenes. American pieces differed from their English counterparts, however, in their simplicity and economy; a minimum of yarn was used and the stitches were simpler.

Measuring 64 by 77 inches, the crewel-embroidered linen bed curtain at left was made in the early 1700s near Boston. Incorporating a tree of life motif, the design features fantastical plants and naturalistic animals, and is expertly executed: different colored yarns provide shading, while a variety of stitches give textural contrast.

The valances are stitched with poignant verses from a pastoral poem.

The flowering trees and flower baskets depicted on the headcloth were common crewel motifs.

These two narrow panels hang by the head of the bed, one on either side.

This curtain, with the one at right, is used at the foot of the bed.

Shaped to fit a particular bed frame, the coverlet features borders of vines.

This foot curtain is similar, but not identical, to its mate at left.

Sometime around 1745, Mary Bulman of York, Maine, began embroidering a set of bed furniture. Her handwork, which includes a coverlet, headcloth, three valances, and four curtains—now displayed on the bed above, at the Old York Historical Society—is the only complete set of American wool-on-linen bedclothes to survive from the 1700s.

Mary's talent with the needle was remarkable. Her exquisite crewelwork coverlet and hangings feature an original design incorporating graceful floral sprays, delicate trees, vines, and birds. Especially notable are the valances, with their finely worked verses taken from the 1706 poem "Meditation in a Grove."

Mary probably began her stitching to occupy her time while her husband served in a campaign against the French in Canada. He died, but her work continued for seven years—through her widowhood and into her second marriage.

Embroidered Blankets

The maker of the circa 1770 embroidered blanket at right devised an imaginative twist on a common theme. Rather than using one flower basket as a central design, she arranged five different baskets along the edges and let the floral sprays spread in profusion over the background.

Almost every colonial household owned at least one wool blanket—sometimes several—and embroidering these textiles was a common occupation by the late 1700s. Becoming popular at a time when making bed rugs and crewelwork hangings was falling from fashion, the practice remained relatively widespread, especially in the more rural areas, into the mid-19th century.

The blankets themselves might be purchased from a professional weaver or made at home. Since the fabrics were produced in widths of no more than thirty-six inches—which was approximately the distance a weaver could throw the shuttle on a hand loom—it was necessary to seam together two or more of these narrow panels to yield a whole bedcover. The wool was generally woven in a solid color or in a plaid

The elegantly worked blanket at left, made in New England in the late 18th century, displays designs closely resembling those found on the crewelwork coverlets that were then fading from fashion. The central floral spray was adapted from the tree of life motif, commonly used in needlework of the period.

pattern; either could serve as an effective background for the embroidered designs.

Often homespun, the yarns were dyed primarily in blues and browns. A wide range of stitches were used, from the simple to the elaborate, but favorite choices included the relatively easy-to-work running and outline stitches. Usually, the decorative needlework on a plain blanket—which might be dyed a dark tint with vegetable colors or left a natural cream-white— ranged across its entire surface. On plaid blankets, which were most frequently white with blue lines, the embroidery was confined within the pattern of squares and often comprised small floral or geometric motifs. A central square or the top border might be reserved for an inscription, such as the date the piece was completed or the maker's name or initials.

In the early 1800s, Hannah Stow of Vermont decorated the colorful, finely woven plaid blanket above
with tiny flower sprigs and diamonds worked in indigo yarn. Her name is stitched along the top edge.

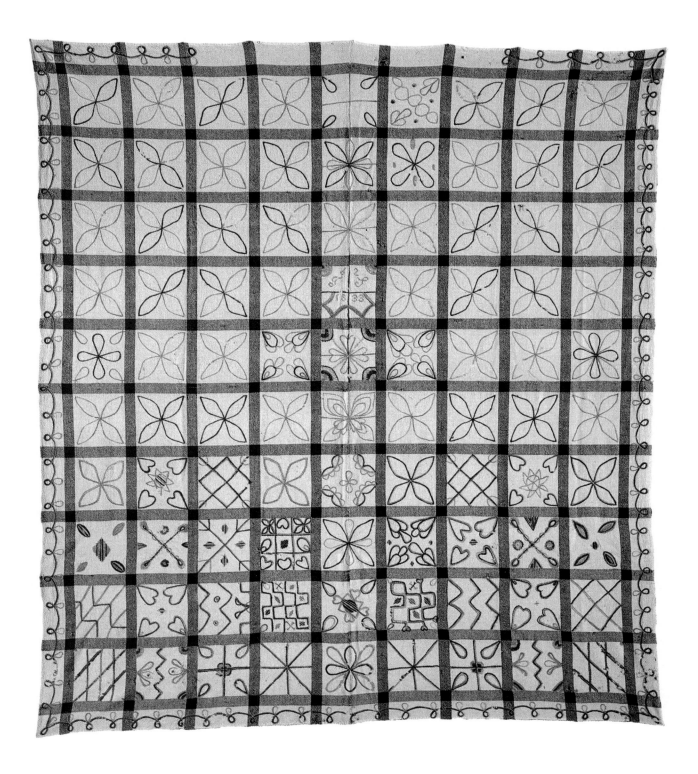

The indigo-dyed plaid blanket above, initialed and dated 1833, is decorated with simply wrought flowers, stars, hearts, and geometric motifs, and is bordered with a running loop design.

Made in Pennsylvania and dated 1831, the blanket above features an array of traditional floral
motifs in a somewhat randomly composed design.

Decorated lavishly and sewn mostly in red yarn—which was not widely available—the circa 1830

blanket above indicates the maker had access to a broad range of dye colors.

THIMBLES AND THIMBLE CASES

Among the most widely collected needlework tools are thimbles, which can be found in a vast range of sizes, shapes, and materials. These familiar and indispensable implements have a remarkably long history: the earliest surviving example—an open-ended metal cylinder dotted with tiny indentations—has been dated to the Han Dynasty in China (AD 100 to 220).

Since that time, thimbles have continued to be made in practically every country of the world for both functional and decorative purposes. The most sought-after examples are generally those handcrafted from such materials as mother-of-pearl, tortoiseshell, enamel, and porcelain, sometimes with precious stones set into their sides. Intended simply to be admired, or used only for sewing delicate fabrics, such fancy thimbles are usually extremely fragile, and those in mint condition are rare.

More common are the thimbles that were mass-produced in the late 19th and early 20th centuries. Although they were turned out in great quantities, these utilitarian, or "workaday" thimbles, made from such durable materials as steel, aluminum, iron, celluloid, and brass, can be surprisingly elaborate. Especially popular with collectors are brass thimbles that display floral patterns, Greek key designs, or the endearing words "Friendship," "Remember," or "Farewell." Also widely collected are silver-clad steel thimbles marked with the trade name "Dorcas." Patented in 1884 by the Englishman Charles Horner and sold in various designs until the 1940s, Dorcas thimbles were hailed as a breakthrough in thimblemaking because they combined the beauty of silver with the durability of steel.

Closely associated with thimbles are the containers that were used to store them. Many resemble eggs, acorns, walnuts, or urns, but more unexpected shapes were also crafted, including hats and slippers, animals, and human figures. Thimble cases made of wood—especially boxwood, rosewood, ebony, mahogany, and various fruitwoods—are the most common, while those fabricated from English silver and French and German porcelain are particularly prized by collectors.

The array of thimbles and thimble cases at right suggests the almost infinite variety available to the collector. Most of these examples date from the 19th and early 20th centuries.

Cotton Counter-panes

Celia Cole had probably seen or made many embroidered pieces before creating the cotton counterpane, signed and dated 1855, at right. Using such common embroidery stitches as the running stitch and the French knot, she worked a variety of traditional designs—including flower baskets, trailing vines, floral sprays, and a central wreath—into a delicate and original composition.

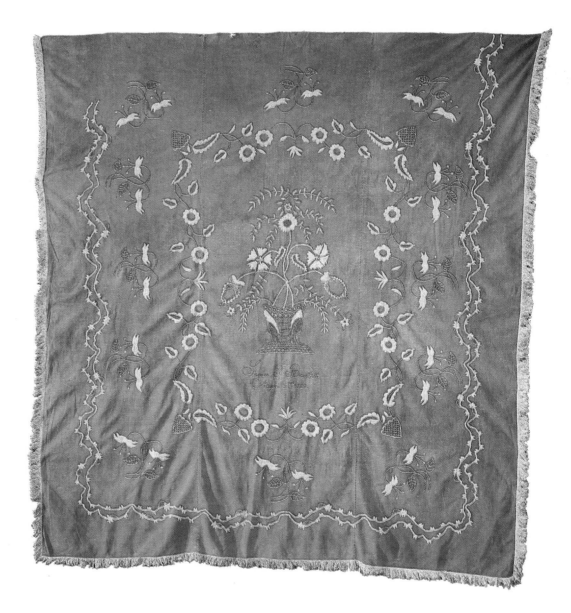

Not all bedcoverings were intended to provide warmth; some were crafted simply as decorative top spreads or as lightweight coverlets for use in summer. In the first half of the 1800s—when cotton fabrics and leisure time became more available—light, pretty top covers, called counterpanes, were especially popular.

Cotton counterpanes were usually embroidered with woolen yarns and most commonly stitched with flower-filled urns and floral vines —the same designs found on woolen blankets. Another popular method used for decorating the bedcovers involved appliqué, in which motifs were cut from separate pieces of cloth and then sewn to a background to form a pattern. This technique was also used to make quilt tops of the period.

The 1827 counterpane above was stitched with white yarn. Although white embroidery, which was popular at the time, was most often worked on a white ground, this piece was done on dyed cotton.

Ann Robinson, who finished the appliquéd counterpane above in 1814, borrowed design elements from varied sources. The central diamond derived from English patchwork quilts, and the trees were adapted from patterns found on printed cottons and crewelwork pieces of the period.

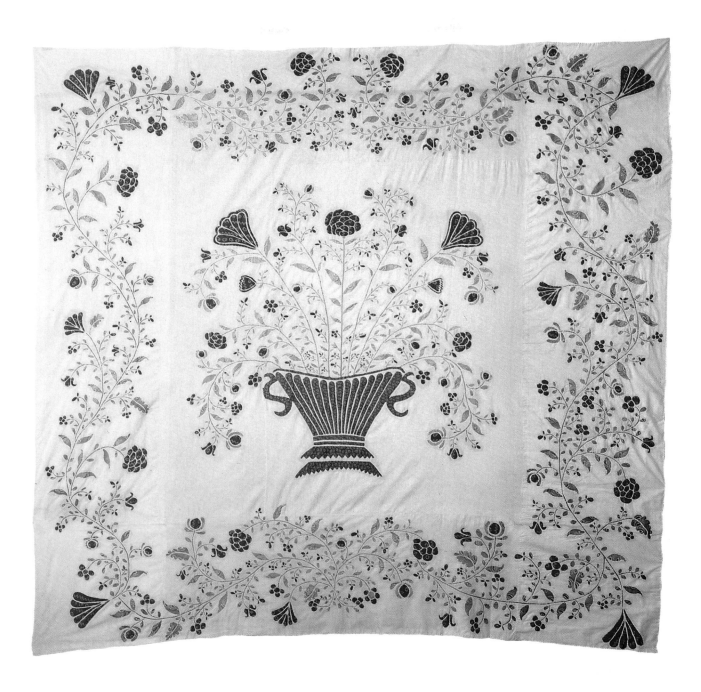

*The maker of the circa 1840 counterpane above was as ambitious as she was talented. She formed part
of the decoration by using the reverse appliqué technique, which required cutting shapes out of the
background and sewing fabric in a contrasting color behind the cutouts.*

The linen candlewick spread above was made in 1825 in Connecticut. The weeping willow was a symbol of mourning.

As a taste for a light, classical look in furnishings developed in the early 19th century, elegant white bedcovers became fashionable. Embroidered with white yarn or thread on a white linen or cotton background, these spreads were found primarily in well-to-do households.

Because color did not enter into the basic design of a whitework spread, texture and shape alone defined the surface pattern, which was slightly raised. This sculptural effect could be achieved with different techniques, among them candlewicking and stuffedwork. The first involved embroidering one layer of cloth with thick cotton thread or yarn that resembled the cord used for candlewicks. The yarn or thread

Whitework Spreads

Appliquéd flowers were used to accent the padded designs on the circa 1850 stuffedwork spread at left. The nautical motifs, including two skillfully wrought clipper ships framed in raised medallions, might signify that the maker lived in a port town.

could be drawn through the fabric to create loops or fringe, or stitched directly onto the fabric to form solid lines. Stuffedwork required a finely woven top and a coarser backing, which were sewn together with decorative needlework. Some of the stitches outlined motifs and created "channels" for padding material, which would be forced bit by bit through small openings made between the threads of the backing. Once the piece was washed, the holes would close up.

Whitework spreads often featured the classical or patriotic symbols fashionable at the time, including urns, grape clusters, swags, cornucopia, and eagles, as well as the traditional floral and star motifs. The most intricate designs could take years to complete.

Creative Quilts

The colorful pomegranates and vines on the circa 1850 cotton quilt at right were common appliqué motifs. By assembling them in a diagonal composition, however, the maker created a unique design. The expert needlework on this piece is particularly evident in the feathers, hearts, and scrolls finely quilted into the "white" spaces.

Among the most common bedcovers in America from the early 19th century to the first decades of the 20th century, quilts could be found in households at every level of society. Quiltmaking served as an art form for many women, who were denied most other avenues of creative self-expression. Depending on the design the maker selected, a quilt could also be used to mark an important event or even to comment on a political or social issue.

While popular, quilts required considerable skill to make, and not everyone could create a successful one. Part of the difficulty lay in the construction. A quilt was typically composed of three layers: a top, most commonly of cotton or wool; a fabric backing; and a filling that might be made of cotton batting, an old bedcover, or combed wool. The components were "sand-

Continued

The quilt top above, appliquéd in the mid-1800s with cotton, silk, and other fabrics, was never finished with a backing. It may have been begun in anticipation of a wedding that did not take place.

More than a thousand tiny hexagons were cut and assembled for the circa 1840 pieced quilt above, made
in Maryland. The Honeycomb pattern was skillfully composed with scraps from roller-printed cottons,
and the quilt was trimmed with a colorful double border of chintz.

The late-19th-century quilt at left exhibits a variation on the Log Cabin pattern. Created by sewing interlocking strips of fabric into blocks, the design was often worked in bright, contrasting colors. The maker of this quilt enhanced the strong optical effect by using yellow fabric at the center of each square.

wiched" together, with tiny, even stitches holding the layers in place. These stitches formed the actual quilting and also served a decorative purpose: worked into patterns, they added a subtle texture and design.

Perhaps the most difficult, yet pleasurable, task was crafting the quilt top. A quiltmaker could choose from the hundreds of traditional patterns that were popular, or invent her own design. One technique used for creating a pattern was appliqué, in which fabric cutouts were stitched onto a quilt top to create an overall design, or were sewn onto fabric squares or "blocks" that were then stitched together.

Piecing scraps together was another common quiltmaking method. Related to the pieced quilt was "crazy" patchwork. This technique developed in the late 1800s and involved stitching irregularly shaped fabric scraps—often remnants of silk and velvet clothing—into blocks that were then sewn onto a backing. Exhibiting erratic patterns and frequently accented with embroidery, crazy quilts reflected the flamboyant taste of the Victorian era.

Scraps cut from old woolen quilts and petticoats were pieced with new fabrics for the quilt above. Richly decorated with embroidery, the bedcover dates to the early or mid-1800s.

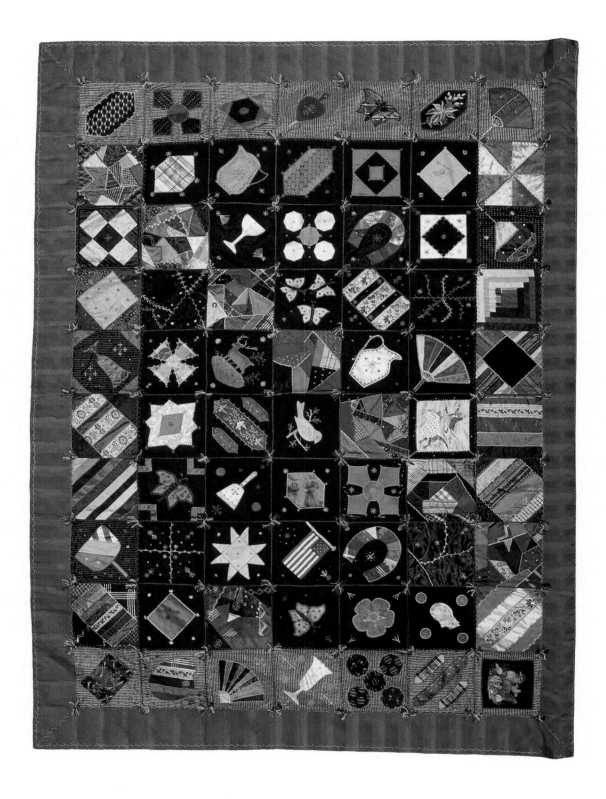

Known as an "album" quilt, the late-19th-century bedcover above, made from silk and satin scraps,

features individual blocks with embroidered and appliquéd "textile pictures."

The circa 1890 crazy quilt above consists of individual appliquéd blocks. The maker effectively selected
textured and printed cottons to represent hair, fur, and other details.

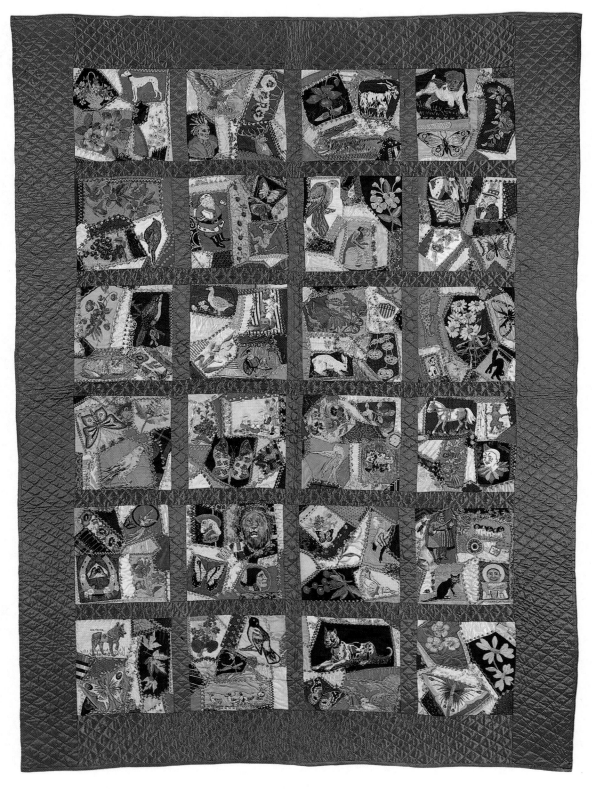

The vividly embroidered quilt above was made in the late 1800s by the American actress Jennie Mackley, who chose remnants of fabrics used to fashion the wardrobe of British royalty.

CRAZYWORK DECOR

In 1884, the editor of *Dorcas Magazine* asserted that "of all the 'crazes' which have swept over and fairly engulfed some of us, there is none which has taken a deeper hold upon the fair women of our land than this one of crazy patchwork."

Lasting from the 1876 Centennial to around 1900, the intense fad for stitching bits of silk and velvet into kaleidoscopic patterns for quilts and accessories came at a time when the Victorian woman was expected to make her home an oasis in an "ugly" world. Ideally, she was to do so by creating an "artistic" environment with her handcrafts, and crazywork proved perfect for the task. The random mix of fabrics characteristic of this patchwork ensured an original look—necessary in "true art"—while the decorative stitching that was worked on such pieces offered the opportunity for suitably elaborate needlework. The striking, asymmetrical patterns, influenced by Japanese design, also satisfied a contemporary taste for the exotic.

As the craftsmanship involved in crazywork was extremely intricate and time consuming, the makers were naturally eager to show off their pieces. Thus, crazywork quilts made the move from bedroom to parlor, where they might be draped over a day bed or piano—in plain view for all to admire. And for those who could not make a large piece, a crazywork chair tidy, table scarf, or ottoman cover would do just as well to embellish a room in proper style.

For the Table

hand-stitched
pieces in embroidery
and appliqué

The needlework featured on the following pages represents some of the distinctly different types of table coverings once fashionable in America. The earliest of these are 18th-century masterpieces in canvaswork that were made strictly for show—not for dining—and would have been found only in affluent households. At the time they were stitched, such table covers were also known as "rugs" or "carpets." These terms originally referred to decorative textiles that were generally placed on a piece of furniture; the notion of a floor rug was still unfamiliar.

Also known as table rugs were the decorative appliquéd coverings popular in the 19th century. Unlike the intricate canvaswork pieces, these fairly simple works in wool or felt did not require difficult stitching, and could be managed—and afforded—by most needleworkers. Equally ubiquitous, silk-embroidered tea cloths, which were all the rage in the late 1800s, reflected a renewed interest in finer stitching, and no self-respecting middle-class housewife would have entertained her friends without one prominently displayed on her tea table.

A detail of an appliquéd penny rug (page 97) shows the fabric circles that make up the colorful surface of such a piece.

Canvaswork Table Covers

Among the most elegant table covers made in early America were those done in canvaswork, the painstaking embroidery fashionable for fine household furnishings and accessories in the 18th century (see also pages 22-27). Stitched in wool or silk, such pieces required time and skill, as well as money for the expensive materials, and the quality workmanship was highly prized.

Done in tent stitch by Mercy Otis of Barnstable, Massachusetts, the intricately worked piece above, depicting playing cards and counters used in the game of loo, was completed sometime before her 1754 wedding to James Warren. The Warrens must have enjoyed considerable status among their contemporaries, for their canvaswork cover was mounted on a Queen Anne card table; such an elegant piece of furniture, designed specifically for gaming, would have been much admired—and found in relatively few households of the time.

The canvaswork table rugs opposite, worked by two sisters from the Oothout family—prominent Dutch settlers in Albany, New York—were made as decorative cloths to be spread over a table or chest, probably in the parlor or "best room." Mary, the elder sister, is thought to have stitched her crewelwork piece, top, in preparation for her marriage, which took place in 1760. Margaret finished her table cover, bottom, in 1764, the year of her own wedding. The pieces are similar in style, suggesting that the two young ladies studied needlework under the same teacher.

The 1759 canvaswork "tablecloath," top, by Mary Oothout, and the 1764 piece, bottom, by Margaret Oothout, were done in crewel wool on linen, primarily in Irish stitch. Such elegant needlework would have properly reflected the social status of the two sisters, from a prominent New York family.

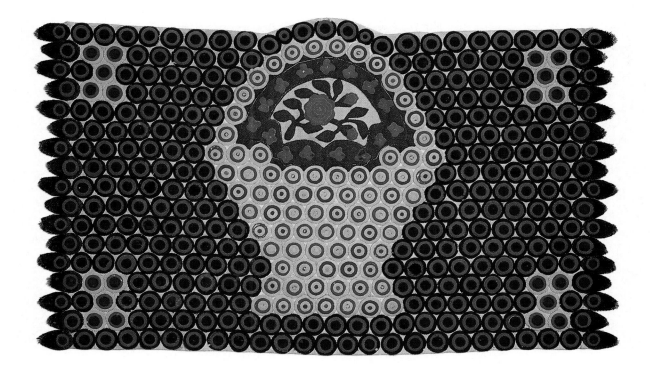

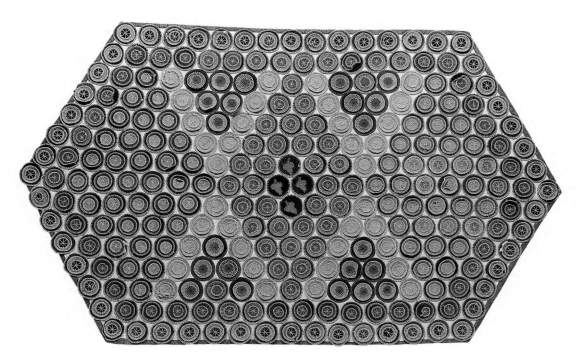

Made around 1860, the table cover at top was appliquéd with wool "pennies" and flower blossoms; its strong pictorial image is rare for a penny rug. More typical is the abstract pattern on the circa 1885 table rug at bottom, which was stitched with fabric cut from worn-out clothing and blankets.

Appliquéd Table Rugs

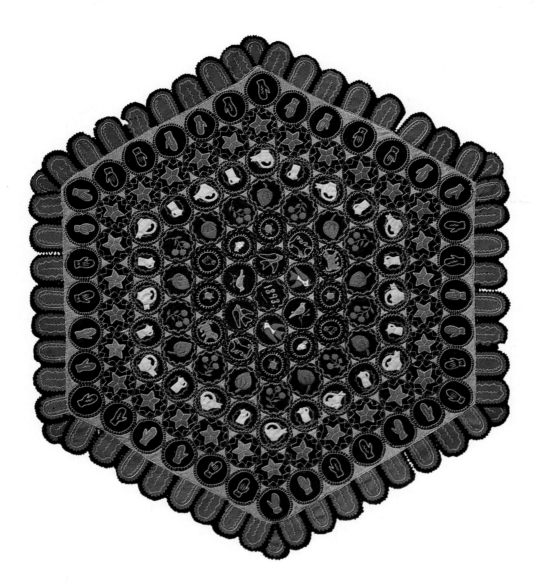

R eaching their peak of popularity around the 1870s, appliquéd table rugs were part of a Victorian fashion for making highly decorative, but largely useless, handicrafts to fill every corner of the home. Pieces like those shown here and on the following pages were not intended for dining. Instead, they were purely ornamental, and might be placed on a parlor table and topped with a vase of flowers, perhaps, or a tasteful arrangement of leather-bound books, to create an "artistic" vignette.

Wool and felt table covers were similar in design and technique to the appliquéd floor rugs and bed covers favored during the same period. Some featured a single overall composition, and others were made with individual "blocks" —as an album quilt would be. The most time-consuming type of appliquéd rug to make was the "penny," or "button," rug, which consisted of hundreds of fabric circles. In these rugs the circles, commonly of woven or felted wool, were traditionally layered and sewn together with buttonhole stitching in sets of three, then mounted on a fabric backing. Further decoration might be added with embroidery or with tiny appliquéd motifs.

The embroidered and appliquéd table rug above, dated 1893, would probably have been used on a round center table, a furniture type popular in the Victorian era.

Red felt was used to appliqué the cotton table rug above, made in the 1860s. The imaginative composition is similar in feeling to that of the circa 1840 wool piece from New York State at right, appliquéd with a variety of cutouts; the two compasses are Masonic symbols.

The circa 1880 velvet table cover above and the early-19th-century piece at left, embellished with crewel embroidery, both feature the kind of overall composition that was typical of such appliquéd works.

The extremely detailed appliquéd piece at right was made by Jane Gove of Wiscasset, Maine, around 1845, shortly after the death of her mother. The eleven-year-old girl is said to have found comfort in creating the composition using fabric cut from her mother's cloth-ing. The finished work, made of wool, measures 74 by 43 inches.

*The appliquéd and embroidered table cover at top, made around 1820 in Otisfield, Maine, depicts a
church, as well as the house where the piece was later discovered. Appliquéd and embroidered "blocks"
were sewn together to make the woolen table rug at bottom, from Norway, Maine.*

Embroidered Tea Cloths

Designs for tea cloths like the silk-embroidered piece above came prestamped on linen backgrounds. The woman who stitched this one, however, personalized it with bands of drawnwork.

Among the household linens that became popular during the late Victorian era were the silk-embroidered cloths that ladies proudly set out when their friends stopped by for afternoon tea.

Embroidered linen tea cloths like those shown here were first stitched around 1895 and reflect the vogue for "art needlework," which had been inspired by a display of British needlework at the 1876 Philadelphia Centennial Exhibition. Art needlework quickly replaced Berlin work (see pages 36-43) because it was considered more "artistic"—requiring freehand stitching and shading techniques that produced a painterly effect. The fad was fueled by the new availability of washable materials and a profusion of books explaining how to do the work. Women could also learn the stitchery by attending special needlework schools set up by museums to teach the principles of "art and design."

As was typical of art needlework, the six tea cloths
at left, all made between
1890 and 1900, feature
realistic, almost painterly,
fruit and flower motifs beautifully shaded in satin stitch.
Embroidered borders
bind the scalloped
edges.

THE DEERFIELD SOCIETY OF BLUE AND WHITE NEEDLEWORK

In 1898, when Ellen Miller and Margaret Whiting, artists who lived in Deerfield, Massachusetts, discovered some 18th-century pieces of crewel embroidery in the town museum, crewelwork had long been out of fashion. At a time when most needlework was done with commercial patterns and materials, the women were extremely impressed by the high quality and originality of the early embroideries. Inspired, they set out to create a record of the deteriorating museum pieces, teaching themselves the stitches that the colonial needleworkers had used, and assembling a portfolio of patterns adapted from early works.

As their own knowledge and needle skills advanced, the two artists found that people were interested not only in buying their work, but also in learning how to do the stitching themselves. Thus, the Deerfield Society of Blue and White Needlework was born; under a cooperative arrangement, Miller and Whiting provided training to the members—who would eventually number about thirty—while allowing them to share in the revenues from the sale of the embroidered doilies, table mats, and other household linens they stitched. Among the first associated groups of craft workers in America, the Society clearly embraced the philosophy of the current Arts and Crafts movement, which advocated a profitable revival of the "honest" handcraftsmanship that had been eclipsed in an industrial age.

In this vein, Society members rejected commercially manufactured materials in favor of those that were handmade. Homespun thread, and

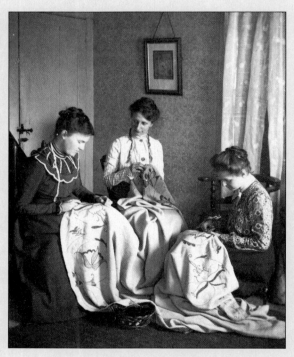

Members of the Deerfield Society of Blue and White Needlework crafting an embroidered coverlet; c. 1900

handwoven linen fabric for the embroidery backgrounds, were purchased, while Miller and Whiting personally produced natural dyes. Even the Society insignia, a "D" inside a spinning wheel, emphasized handcraftsmanship.

Based on some of the museum pieces, the early embroideries stitched by Miller and Whiting were done in indigo-dyed blue thread on natural linen backgrounds (inspiring the name of the Society), but other colors were introduced almost immediately. Not intended as replicas, the new works showed many departures from 18th-century crewelwork traditions. Notably, Society pieces were done in linen thread rather than the less durable wool that their predecessors had used. Also, as artists, Miller and Whiting were quite interested in creating original work of their own. As well as producing historically based designs, they devised many new patterns, a number of which reflected the current vogue for art nouveau. Even their stitches were not always traditional; Deerfield Society pieces, for example, were frequently done in cross-stitch, which was not typical of colonial embroidery.

Embraced by the Deerfield community, where a number of artists lived, the Deerfield Society prospered for thirty years. Its work was exhibited to acclaim, and drew crowds of buyers. During the First World War, however, output decreased as the women turned their energies to rolling bandages and knitting socks to help the war effort. As interest in the needlework waned after the war, there were fewer orders, and in 1926 the aging founders regretfully disbanded the Society.

A cross-stitch pattern, a departure
from early crewelwork designs; c. 1905

An art nouveau dragonfly pattern
worked on blue-dyed linen; c. 1910

A satin stitch design, seldom found in
Deerfield pieces; c. 1900

A traditional 18th-century embroidery design stitched in blue and white; c. 1900

A stylized floral design adapted from
an 18th-century embroidery; 1890s

Art nouveau poppies in herringbone,
feather, and outline stitches; 1899

Handcrafted Rugs

an imaginative range of
coverings for the floor

With the exception of woven straw mats and painted canvas cloths, floor rugs were uncommon in America until the 1800s. Affluent households might boast an imported Oriental or Brussels carpet, but the majority of the population lived with bare wood floors; after the boards were scoured with water, it was customary to sprinkle on a layer of white sand (good for absorbing grease and moisture) that would be swept into decorative designs.

Just why the idea of floor rugs took so long to catch on is unclear, but once it did, needleworkers began turning out homemade versions by the hundreds. While not everyone could afford a manufactured carpet, anybody with fabric remnants, some extra yarn, or worn-out clothing on hand could use the scraps to make their own colorful rugs. While such pieces helped ward off drafts and were quite practical, they could also be exceptionally beautiful.

Shirring, seen in a detail from a circa 1830 rug (page 114), was an appliqué
technique often used in 19th-century rugmaking.

Yarn-Sewn Rugs

Distorted perspective only enhances the charm of the circa 1800 yarn-sewn rug above, made with brightly colored yarns stitched onto a linen backing.

Among the earliest fabric floor coverings crafted in America were yarn-sewn rugs, produced primarily between about 1800 and 1840. Worked in the same manner as bed rugs (see pages 58-63), such coverings were made by sewing two-ply yarn through a loosely woven backing—a piece of linen, perhaps, or an old grain sack—in a continuous running stitch to form loops. The looping followed the shape of the various motifs of the rug design, and was usually clipped to create a soft pile.

Typically about four feet long and only two or three feet wide, yarn-sewn rugs were sometimes designed as table covers, but are also believed to have been used extensively as hearthrugs, or "fire rugs." In households fortunate enough to have an imported Oriental or manufactured carpet, the small yarn-sewn rugs served as protection from flying sparks, and made decorative hearth coverings when the fireplace was cold. Relatively few 19th-century yarn-sewn rugs survive, because the materials were so fragile; those that do exist are thought to have been made in northern New England.

Flowers and flower baskets, such as those on the circa 1830 wool-on-linen rugs above, were among the most common designs stitched into yarn-sewn rugs. The piece at top features a distinctive striped border, and the one at bottom is decorated with fringe, a less traditional treatment.

The design of the yarn-sewn rug at top is personal in nature, while that of the piece at bottom has a patriotic theme. The stars on the latter probably represent the seventeen states of the Union, suggesting that the rug was made after 1803 and before 1820, when the eighteenth state was admitted.

The scene on the Maine rug at top may have been inspired by a broadside for a menagerie that was
traveling in New England around the time the circa 1834 piece was made. The Bengal tiger, bottom,
was probably adapted from an illustration in Thomas Bewick's 1820 History of Quadrupeds.

Geometric motifs are much rarer than pictorial themes on yarn-sewn floor coverings. The rugs above,
found in southern Maine, were probably the work of the same maker and feature
vibrantly colored squares, circles, and diamonds.

CARE OF ANTIQUE RUGS

More fragile than many antiques, old rugs require special care to preserve their easily damaged fibers. If shopping for a rug, buy one that is in good condition, without stains. When squeezed lightly, the textile should feel supple, not dry; a rug that is dried out will be brittle and may shed powdery flakes, caused by the breakdown of the backing.

Professional conservators should be consulted about major restoration problems, but general care of a rug in good condition can be undertaken at home. Never shake or beat an antique rug or put it in a washing machine, as such treatment can damage the backing and dislodge fibers. To clean the rug, sweep it lightly with a soft brush. Vacuuming the top—but not the backing—is also acceptable for removing loose dirt, so long as the rug is protected with a clean piece of fiber-glass screening.

If a rug requires washing and can withstand it, the textile should first be tested for colorfastness by wetting a small area with a little cold water. Blot the area with a white cloth; if the dye does not bleed onto the cloth, the fibers should be colorfast. Next, dip a sponge in cold water mixed with mild detergent and squeeze it almost dry. To clean the rug, dab or gently rub the surface with the sponge in a circular motion, then rinse by sponging with cold water; avoid wetting the backing.

As a last resort, a heavily soiled rug can be soaked. Use cold, soapy water, and leave the rug immersed no longer than one hour. Loosen the dirt with a sponge or brush, but do not agitate the rug; rinse the piece well in cold water. Take special care when handling a wet rug: the added weight of the water can cause the piece to tear if it is not supported properly. Do not wring or squeeze a wet rug, or hang one on a line. Instead, blot the rug by rolling it in a towel with the front side out. Unroll the rug, then lay it flat, turning it over periodically as it dries.

An antique rug should not be exposed to excessive wear or direct sun. To protect the backing, place a synthetic-fiber pad beneath the piece. If storing the rug, do not fold it; lay it flat or roll it loosely, front side out. Keep it in a sheet or towel—never in a plastic bag—in a clean, dark, dry place where the temperature remains around 70 degrees.

Shirred Rugs

The large circa 1830 caterpillar-shirred woolen rug above, which measures 56 by 64 inches, was cleverly pieced together in sections to create the complex overall design.

Shirred rugs are thought to have become popular in the 1830s. At this time, inexpensive woolen and cotton fabrics were being manufactured at mills across New England, and it was customary to save remnants for use in making decorative furnishings. Because the cloth was too thick to be sewn through a backing—as yarn could be—a number of methods for applying scraps onto a foundation were developed for rugmaking.

The most common method was known as caterpillar, or chenille, shirring, in which cloth strips were gathered into "caterpillars" that were then sewn onto a fabric backing so that the puckered strips created a crinkled effect.

In another method, known as bias shirring, narrow strips of cloth were cut on the bias and folded lengthwise. The folded edges were sewn to the rug backing so that the raw edges, closely packed next to each other, formed a pile; small squares or circles might also be bunched in a similar method, called patch shirring. The least common, and most demanding, of these appliqué techniques, however, was pleated shirring, in which cloth strips were folded, then stitched to the backing in tight, accordian-like ribbons.

*The 12-by-10-foot caterpillar-shirred rug above, in cotton and silk on a linen backing, was made
between 1825 and 1850. Because furniture in that period was customarily placed along the walls,
a large rug like this one would have been a prominent centerpiece in a room.*

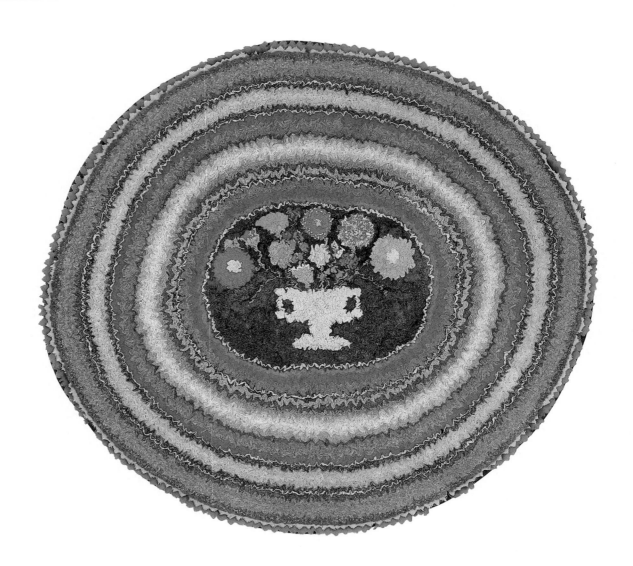

The caterpillar shirring method was skillfully used on these two rugs to make the simple floral motifs come alive. On the rare circular piece above, made around 1840, the urn is surrounded by radiating rings; on the rug at right, the flowers seem to ripple against the wavy background.

These two shirred rugs, with
their wild, colorful profusion of flowers, are veritable
gardens for the floor. The
circa 1850 example above
was done on a linen
foundation and features an
urn-and-flowers design
typical of the period. Wool
fabric strips were used
for the shirring on the circa
1855 rug at left, backed
with cotton ticking.

The horse's coat on the circa 1845 bias-shirred rug at top shows how fabric colors might be blended. The circa 1830 rug at bottom was made with bias and caterpillar shirring; the backing was cut from a patchwork quilt completed earlier in the century.

The late-19th-century Shaker rug, top, with a sprightly though misshapen horse framed in the center, was made with patch shirring. Bunched fabric circles were sewn onto the backing, then a braided border was added. Pleated shirring was used to create the crisply detailed rug at bottom.

Hooked Rugs

Although they were made almost a century apart, the hooked rugs shown here are remarkably similar. The circa 1840 piece above is one of the earliest known floor coverings of this type and has a homespun hemp backing. The Grenfell rug, right, was made around 1920; the urn-and-flower design is seldom seen on these Canadian rugs.

Probably the most familiar of early American floor coverings are hooked rugs, which were made by pulling rag strips—with a hook—up through a woven foundation to create a dense pile. Hooked rugs were produced primarily after the 1830s, when it was discovered that the burlap sacking used for shipping goods from overseas was an excellent foundation fabric for rugs. Although hemp and linen were also used for backing, the jute fiber in burlap was stronger, and the weave looser, making it easy to pull the fabric strips through.

While hooking rugs was common practice from the second half of the 1800s into the early 20th century, the exact origins of the craft are unclear. It was once thought that hooked rugs evolved from the fabric-strip rugs that were made in rural England as early as 1800, yet those pieces were not worked with a hook. The tool used for American hooked rugs is thought to have been adapted from a device used in rope making—which supports the theory that these rugs developed around coastal New England and the maritime provinces of Canada. From there, it appears, the fashion for hooking pieces spread across the country.

While certain motifs, such as flowers and animals, recur frequently in hooked rugs and are usually represented in a literal way, the overall compositions have their own, often idiosyncratic, character. Proportions are sometimes distorted—a bird might be rendered the same size as the tree on which it perches, or figures and buildings flattened into two dimensions. Even after prestamped rug backings became available in the 1860s through peddlers and catalogs, many

Continued

The maker of the 1885 hooked rug above created a sculptured effect by clipping the pile to varying lengths. Both the three-dimensional surface and the oval wreath pattern are typical of Waldoboro rugs, which are thought to have been made around that southern Maine town.

The circa 1880 hooked rug above, made with woolen yarns and rag strips, was done in the
Log Cabin pattern, also used for quilts. The maker faithfully reproduced the blocks of concentric squares
and eye-popping optical illusions that characterize the pattern.

makers continued to develop original compositions, or adapted the prepared patterns to their own tastes, so that these rugs also tend to have a distinctive look.

The designs hooked into rugs derived from a variety of sources. Quilt patterns—especially geometric favorites such as the Log Cabin—for example, were frequently adapted for these coverings. Popular engravings and book illus-trations also provided design sources. Because hooking was primarily a rural craft, many pieces bear scenes inspired by country life—pastoral landscapes, bustling villages, or farmyards complete with horses, chickens, and sheep. Still other examples display bizarre combinations of images and symbols that could only have sprung from the most uninhibited of imaginations.

Certain rug patterns and styles are also associ-

Continued

Made in Pennsylvania around 1870, the hooked rug above features a colorful abstract pattern. The painterly composition is "framed" with a border of braided rag strips.

Known as cobblestones or lambs' tongues, the designs on the circa 1920 hooked rug above were probably created by tracing part way around a saucer or plate.

ated with specific locations. Waldoboro rugs, which feature irregularly sheared pile, are named for a small town in Maine—although it is uncertain whether the type actually originated there. Grenfell rugs, from Canada's Labrador peninsula, are named in honor of Dr. Wilfred Grenfell, who founded a mission and promoted rug hook-

ing, and other cottage industries, as a way for impoverished families in the area to generate extra income. Sold primarily through the mission from 1900 to 1930, Grenfell rugs are noted for their soft colors, tight, smooth hooking, and distinctively northern subject matter, often inspired by local fauna, such as polar bears and puffins.

Abstract cloud patterns characterize the late-19th-century cotton and wool hooked rug at top. The unusual hooked rug at bottom, made in the 1920s or 1930s of rayon and cotton, features tufted dots arranged in a geometric pattern.

The whimsical designs on these two late-19th-century hooked rugs raise intriguing questions about the characters' relationships. Is the stout cat at top stalking rabbit prey or befriending a fellow household pet? What does the size reversal of the giant chicken and dwarfed man, bottom, indicate?

The pink-bellied fish portrayed on the late-19th-century hooked rug at top may have been meant as a consolation prize for a fisherman who lost his catch. The unusual scene on the early-20th-century Grenfell rug, bottom, is thought to depict a hunt; the squares probably represent whales or seals.

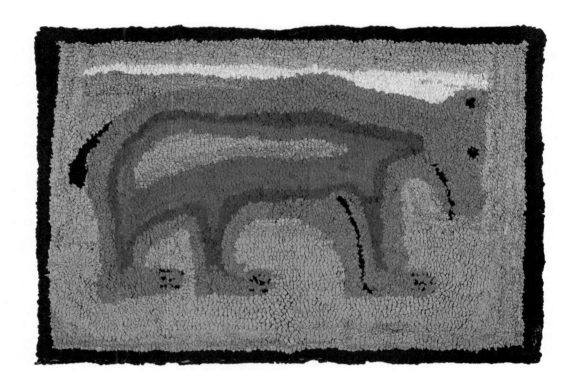

Animals, both wild and domestic, were favorite subjects for rug hookers, although the designs were not always literal renderings. The bear on the circa 1910 rug above was worked in bright reds and pinks, while the horse on the circa 1930 rug at right boasts an interesting haircut.

The maker of the circa 1880 hooked rug above attempted to show off the markings—and perhaps the hunting abilities—of her calico cat. The choice of colors may have been intentional, but probably just reflect a use of fabrics that were on hand. The whimsical piece at left was made in southeastern Pennsylvania; makers began working dates into hooked rugs around 1895.

Unconventional design brings a sense of vitality to these hooked pieces. The distorted "aerial" view on the circa 1900 rug above results in a unique composition. The 75-inch-long rug at right, hooked around 1870, teems with a kaleidoscopic "zoo" that features snakes, birds, cats, dogs, a mule, and a horse.

Made around 1885 by the wife of a Baltimore fisherman, the hooked rug at top includes a giant fish and fisherman's knot floating in the sky. Thought to be a wedding rug, the circa 1900 piece at bottom shows a mysterious moon, a groom, and a bride—standing on her own tiny rug.

The circa 1885 hooked rug above, made by Mrs. Eleanor Blackstone of Illinois, using yarn, cloth, and strands of her children's hair, depicts each of her six offspring involved in a favorite pastime.

The hooked rug at top, featuring a schoolyard scene (viewed by four rabbits in the bottom left corner), was made in Massachusetts at the turn of the century. Lucy Barnard of Dixfield Common, Maine, hooked a scene featuring her house and a favorite horse, Betsy, on the rug at bottom around 1860.

THE RUGS OF EDWARD FROST

The finished rugs, right, show two variations on the catalog drawing above. The rugmakers used different colored fabrics, changing the design slightly to suit their own tastes.

One evening in 1868, Edward Sands Frost, a tin peddler and machinist from Maine, noticed a new needlework project his wife had begun: she was hooking a rug. Intrigued, Frost sat down to help with the task himself, and by the time the piece was finished he had decided that he could improve on the design. His supposition was indeed correct, and within two years he had stopped peddling tin and become the country's first commercial producer of hooked rug patterns, maintaining a shop in Biddeford, Maine, and a branch office in Boston at a store by the name of Gibbs & Warren.

Frost's earliest designs, peddled door to door from his cart, were hand-drawn. Orders came in so fast, however, that the entrepreneur soon turned to stenciling as a means of mass-production, cutting his first templates from scrap tin in his stable. Eventually, Frost had some 750 templates, most made of zinc, that were used in various combinations to stencil more than 180 different designs

in color onto burlap backgrounds; the pieces to be made ranged from chair seats to rugs measuring nine feet long.

While some of the Frost designs were original, many were copied or adapted from finished rugs that Frost acquired, through barter or purchase, on his travels along the back roads of Maine. The majority displayed floral or animal themes, but patriotic and Masonic symbols, and a variety of geometric motifs, also appeared; among his most unusual patterns were a group imitating imported Oriental rugs.

Frost retired in 1876, selling his business to James A. Strout, who continued to produce the rug patterns until 1900 under the name E. S. Frost & Co. It was probably Strout who recorded the designs in the illustrated catalogs that started to become available at about this time; it is thought that shops kept such catalogs on hand so that needleworkers could choose their patterns from the numbered designs.

The catalog drawing, near right, shows a reclining spaniel surrounded by a floral wreath; the needleworker who hooked the finished rug, far right, added a braided border of her own design.

By using various stencils, Frost was able to produce elaborate colored patterns on burlap backings like the one at left. The maker hooked directly over the pattern, filling in with her own fabric scraps.

The Lion and Palm design, shown in the catalog drawing far left, was one of Frost's most popular. The maker of the rug at left faithfully followed the design, but chose to work a simpler border.

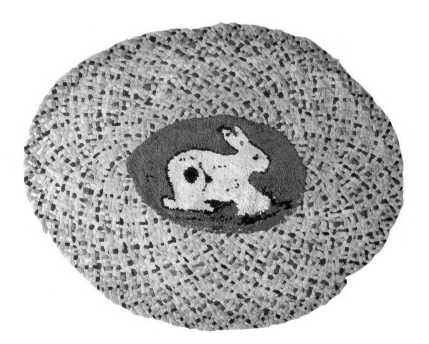

The imaginative needleworker who made the rug at top around 1850 appliquéd a braided floral design

onto a braided background; this is one of only two such rugs known to exist. The wool rug at bottom,

made in the late 1800s or early 1900s, combines hooking with braiding.

Braided, Knitted, and Crocheted Rugs

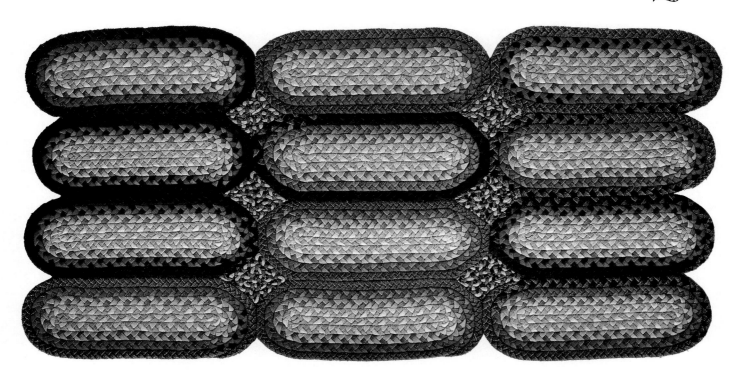

Braided, knitted, and crocheted floor coverings, like all rag rugs, were devised to make use of fabric and yarn scraps. Despite the fact that they were fashioned from odds and ends, however, such pieces were often very carefully composed with regard to color patterns and textures—making them all the more remarkable for their workmanship and design.

Although braided rugs are mentioned in colonial records, they were apparently not prevalent until the 1800s. They were crafted simply by plaiting strips of fabric into a thick band; the band was then wrapped around itself, with more braiding added as necessary. Ovals and circles were the most common shapes because they were the easiest to form.

Knitted and crocheted rugs were popular from the mid- to late 1800s, and again in the early 1900s as part of a general revival of American handcrafts. These durable, colorful, washable— and reversible—floor mats were crafted with yarn or fabric. Narrow bands would be worked on knitting needles or with a crochet hook and then sewn together in strips, or wound around themselves in the same way that a braided rug was formed.

The maker of the early-20th-century rug above created an unusual piece by joining twelve braided ovals to make a larger composition.

*The braided rug at top, from New England, probably dates from the early 1900s and was worked
in wool. The rug at bottom is of wool and cotton with an appliquéd border.*

The dazzling room-sized wool-and-cotton rug above, made in the early 1900s, incorporates small and large braided circles into a geometrically patterned hooked background.

Typical of many Shaker handcrafts, the knitted rug above, made around 1890, was superbly designed and executed. Each section contains at least two colors, providing added brilliance and depth, while each outer strip features geometric figures, such as crosses, diamonds, checkerboards, and chevrons.

The early-1900s Amish rug at top features braided and crocheted borders around crocheted stars.

The crocheted rug at bottom, also Amish, has a center panel made with cloth from old dresses.

Known as the Caswell carpet, the embroidered rug above was the ambitious undertaking of Vermont needleworker Zeruah Higley Guernsey Caswell. Measuring some 162 square feet and dated 1835, it is an original creation.

The Caswell Carpet

Zeruah Higley Guernsey was not yet thirty years old when she undertook one of the most remarkable—and one of the few known—embroidered floor coverings to be stitched in early America. Begun around 1832 and marked with the date 1835, Zeruah's room-sized carpet was designed for her father's parlor and measures approximately 13½ by 12 feet; its size alone is a testament

to the monumental task the piece represents.

Few of Zeruah's contemporaries would have been willing to commit themselves to the work required for such an ambitious project. Moreover, at the time the needleworker made her carpet, householders who could afford them were purchasing manufactured floral-patterned carpets from England and France. Perhaps Zeruah's embroidered rug was her own homemade version of one she could not buy.

Although Zeruah, who lived in the small town of Castleton in northern Vermont, enlisted the help of others in her project, she herself participated in every step of its production. Her own sheep, given to her for the purpose, provided the wool, which

was spun, dyed, and woven at home.

Made up of individual sections—seventy-seven in all—the piece is composed in much the same way an album quilt would be. Each block, of twill-weave wool, was embroidered in chain stitch with a different design. Most of the precise, stylized patterns are variations on floral themes, including flower-filled urns and sprays of blossoms. There are also birds, as well as hearts, a shell, and a butterfly. At the top edge of the carpet, Zeruah added her monogram above six blue blossoms; under the leaves of the plant are stitched "LFM." A block near the right edge is marked "By FB." These last two sets

of initials are thought to be those of two young Potawatomi Indians who studied at the local medical college and boarded in town; the students

apparently worked on the rug, each contributing a design.

Especially notable among the different blocks are three that depict household pets, all of which are seated on striped rag carpets—the more usual floor coverings of the day. A somewhat mysterious block

features the figures of a man and woman, whose identities remain unknown. The lady and her swain evidently had some private meaning for Zeruah, for the needleworker concealed the block by stitching another panel over it; the design was only discovered years later by a subsequent owner of the carpet. Particularly remarkable for its workmanship is the detachable hearth panel, stitched with a basket of flowers and framed by a red sawtooth border, that would be removed when the fireplace was in use.

Zeruah Guernsey married in 1846, becoming Mrs. Caswell, and set up her new home, where she placed the rug on her parlor floor. Although the room was seldom used, it is said that Mrs. Caswell was always willing to allow callers to view, and inevitably admire, her masterpiece.

Needlework in the Home

the pleasures of living with

a collection

Collectors become intrigued with needlework for many reasons. Some are attracted to beautifully designed quilts and hooked rugs as original works of folk art. Others might be fascinated by the quality of craftsmanship that is represented in early embroidery and other types of stitchery. Still others enjoy needlework for the warmth and color it can bring to a room.

This chapter features three houses, ranging in date from the 17th to the 19th centuries, in which antique bed covers, rugs, and embroideries play a central role in the decor. Shown off to advantage on walls, furniture, and floors, the textiles have been used effectively as artwork, and blend easily with their surroundings. While all of the collectors stress the importance of caring properly for such pieces, they also take enormous pleasure in keeping their needlework out on display; using the textiles makes it possible to enjoy them every day.

Nineteenth-century needlework pieces, including hooked rugs, pieced quilts, a woven coverlet, and an appliquéd table rug used as a wall hanging, bring color to a bedroom.

Collecting by Design

The silkwork picture above, draped over a settee, was stitched in Montgomery County, Pennsylvania, in the 1880s. The embroidered velvet and ostrich-feather fan next to it dates to around 1820, and the New England paint-decorated darner is from the mid-1800s.

It was the colorful imagery of hooked rugs that initially drew the owners of this 1830s house in the small town of Erwinna, Pennsylvania, to American needlework and textiles. "We've always collected by eye," emphasize the homeowners. "When we're searching for pieces, particular regions or historical periods are never as important to us as good design."

The impact of that design is evident throughout their comfortable house, where hooked rugs are by no means the only eye-catching textiles to be found. In addition, there are pieced and embroidered quilts, embroidered blankets, fine-

Continued

In the living room, right, a successful mix of pieces includes a late-1800s Pennsylvania coverlet, above the mantel, and a crocheted rug made around 1930 in North Carolina.

ly stitched samplers and needlework pictures, woven coverlets, appliquéd table rugs, and brightly colored crocheted rugs—all of which are treated as pieces of art in an expressive and ever-changing display.

Found in nearly every room of the house, the striking needlework and textiles seem made for exhibition. "Virtually from the time we began collecting," say the couple, "we responded to the pieces as pictures." They find the hooked rugs particularly compelling because they exhib-

it the imaginative artistry of the 19th-century women who made them—frequently from their own designs. "It may not have been widely accepted for a woman to be a painter," the couple explain, "but in making a rug she could create anything she wished and the results would be favorably regarded."

The couple's interest in hooked designs in turn helped them to discover the other types of needlework that they now collect, as well as accessories and some of the tools that were tradi-

Continued

The hearts, birds, and pinwheels on the embroidered table rug, shown above and on the dining table at

left, have a distinctly Pennsylvania-German look. The piece was sewn as a sampler by a child from

Bucks County in the mid- or late 19th century. The appliquéd table cover with a squirrel design was

made in Lancaster County around 1900, and now is used effectively as a wall hanging.

Among the 19th-century rugs displayed in the bedroom at right is an 1840s wool-on-linen caterpillar-shirred piece, mounted on the wall. The rugs on the floor were hooked in New England; the one to the right of the bed was based on a quilt pattern and resembles the blocks in the bed quilt, which is from Bucks County, Pennsylvania.

The quilt draped on the sofa at far left was made by Rebecca Cliffton Hampton in 1852. The details from the quilt, at near left, show the pieced border with her signature block (top); the overall Tumbling Blocks pattern (center); and the glazed cotton backing and unusual checkered binding (bottom). Rebecca was twelve years old when she made her quilt; she died of consumption a year later.

Twentieth-century
needlework pieces are put to
use in the nursery, right.
The brightly colored
appliquéd summer coverlet
folded on the rocker was
made in the 1930s, as was
the embroidered crib
blanket.

tionally used in needlework. By choosing pieces that are all graphically bold—strong in color and simple in design—the couple found that it was quite easy to combine works successfully, even though their collection mixes an extensive variety of types, patterns, and styles from all over the country.

Because they purchase only pieces that are in good condition, the collectors feel comfortable making use of them on the floors, walls, and beds throughout their home, although they caution that care should be taken when hanging any textile, to make sure the fibers do not sag or break. Whenever possible, they also try to find out as much as they can about the family history of a piece. Knowing, for instance, the name of the person who made a quilt, where she lived, and how old she was when she did the stitching adds to their joy in living with the quilt today.

However charming the history or lovely the craftsmanship of any piece, their decision to bring home a quilt, a rug, or an embroidered work always comes back to the strength of its individual design. And once they own a piece, the collectors give considerable thought to finding the right place for its display, allowing each object an uncluttered space of its own. "To us, all of our needlework is art," the collectors say. "We want every piece to stand out."

Embroidered baby blankets were popular needlework projects between the 1880s and 1930s. While some blankets came prestamped with designs, the Alice in Wonderland patterns above, all from the crib blanket opposite, are thought to have been drawn by the embroiderer.

A Respect
for Fine
Stitchery

The living room, right, is a showplace for finely stitched needlework pictures. Two mid-18th-century canvaswork Fishing Lady pictures hang above the fireplace, and between them is an Adam and Eve sampler made in Boston around 1750. To the right of the fireplace is a silk-on-gauze picture of Rachel and Jacob, stitched by a Massachusetts schoolgirl around 1772.

The couple who restored this 1685 Connecticut farmhouse have long admired fine workmanship and have a personal interest in crafts. One has taught spinning, weaving, and embroidery; the other is accomplished in papermaking, bookbinding, and woodturning. It was only natural that the two, working together as antiques dealers, would eventually focus on early needlework as their specialty.

The embroidered pictures, samplers, and accessories, such as canvaswork pocketbooks, displayed in the house date from the 1600s to about 1830. The pieces are well suited to the low-ceilinged rooms of the old building, where they are set off by simple paneling and whitewashed walls, and complemented by a collection of early-18th-century New England furniture.

Among the homeowners' most prized embroideries are several canvaswork scenes, known as

Continued

The framed silk-on-linen sampler above was made by a schoolgirl in Norwich, Connecticut, around 1774. Unlike the backgrounds of most samplers, this one is completely filled in with cross-stitching. A collection of 18th-century canvaswork pocketbooks is displayed on the table below.

The canvaswork picture above is thought to have been designed by Susannah Condy in Boston around 1740. On the table are a queen-stitched purse made around 1820, and a fichu, or triangular scarf, of embroidered cotton gauze.

Fishing Lady pictures (see page 23 for more information). Stitched in silk and wool on extremely fine-meshed canvas, they are believed to have been designed by Susannah Condy, a needlework teacher in Boston in the mid-1700s, and exhibit painstaking workmanship.

Other remarkable treasures include a box decorated with stumpwork, or raised embroidery, which was made by a 17th-century lady of the English court, and a queen-stitched purse made in America around 1820.

As was typical of the all-purpose "halls" in 17th-century dwellings, the room at right contains a bed. The crewel-embroidered coverlet was made in Connecticut around 1740.

An Eye for Comfort

A striking collection of quilts and hooked rugs provides both color and pattern throughout the rooms of this house, where the early American textiles are compatible with the clean lines of contemporary furniture and simple country antiques.

The 1789 house was moved from Massachusetts to its present site on Long Island by the current owners, who added a kitchen ell and an updated keeping room in the process. From the start of the project, the two owners wanted the decor simply to "flow," so the house would

An 1880s pieced quilt in the Drunkard's Path pattern makes a colorful throw for the sofa in the living room, left. The design of the mid-19th-century hooked rug over the fireplace, with its moon, stars, and flowers, is a delightfully abstract reference to nature.

be comfortable and easy to maintain. More-over, as antiques dealers who have specialized in quilts for over twenty years, they also knew they wanted American needlework to have an important place in the decorative scheme.

Ultimately, they chose antique furniture for the early rooms while including some more modern pieces in the newer wing; their quilts and rugs, however, appear in both areas of the house and act as a connecting link between old and new. "Many people who like needlework of this type also enjoy contemporary design," say

Continued

The crib quilt on the wall, above, was probably made by Louisa's grandmother. The friendship quilt on the bed is signed by its makers.

the homeowners. "We find that the antique and new pieces work well together visually, with quilts and rugs providing a softening element."

The remarkable qualities of quilts in particular have a very strong appeal for many people, the collectors have observed. Because the hand-stitched pieces represent love and hard work, they believe, people tend to associate quilts with feelings of solace and comfort. And when the fabric colors become soft and mellow with age, the textiles convey the sense that they have been much used and cared for over the years.

In fact, all of the needlework pieces that these two collectors bring home to live with are chosen precisely because they are "lovable," not because they are rare finds or major showpieces. Each seems to have some irresistible characteristic, be it the tiny size of the doll clothes that the owners have mounted and displayed behind glass, or simply the familiarity of favorite quilt designs, such as the Drunkard's Path or Sawtooth patterns, stitched by mothers and daughters through many generations.

Indeed, it is the endless variety of quilt pat-

Continued

Pieced from a variety of fabrics, the 19th-century bedcover on the banquette above was worked in the Sawtooth pattern.

An early-20th-century hooked rug depicting a bird is displayed as artwork over the bedroom fireplace, above.

terns that is fascinating to these collectors, as is the diversity of fabrics that make up the appliquéd and pieced coverlets. "Some quilts contain bits of cloth that span fifty years in date," they say. "You might see dark-colored chintzes of the early 1800s and the pretty little French-inspired prints that were introduced a bit later, as well as Victorian silks—all in a single quilt." It would be difficult not to be interested in such a piece, knowing that the needleworker who made it

Continued

A New England owl rug hooked in the early 1900s and a 19th-century bedcover stitched with crewel embroidery distinguish the bedroom at right.

The doll clothes framed and
hung over the bedroom
fireplace at right date to the
Civil War period. The bright
appliquéd quilt on the bed
was probably made
a little earlier.

had been carefully saving and recycling fabrics and remnants for decades.

Because of their particular interest in quilts, the pair do not limit the use of such pieces to traditional display on a bed; they also use them as effective accents—thrown casually on a sofa, perhaps, or folded over a quilt rack to brighten the corner of a room, or mounted on a wall as a striking "graphic." Together with the equally eye-catching hooked rugs that have their own places throughout the house, the pieces create an overall effect that is comfortable, friendly, and welcoming.

The tree of life needlework picture above, appliquéd with crocheted figures, is thought to have been made in Tennessee in the late 19th century. The animal dolls are new, but their clothes were made with antique fabrics.

Needlework Techniques

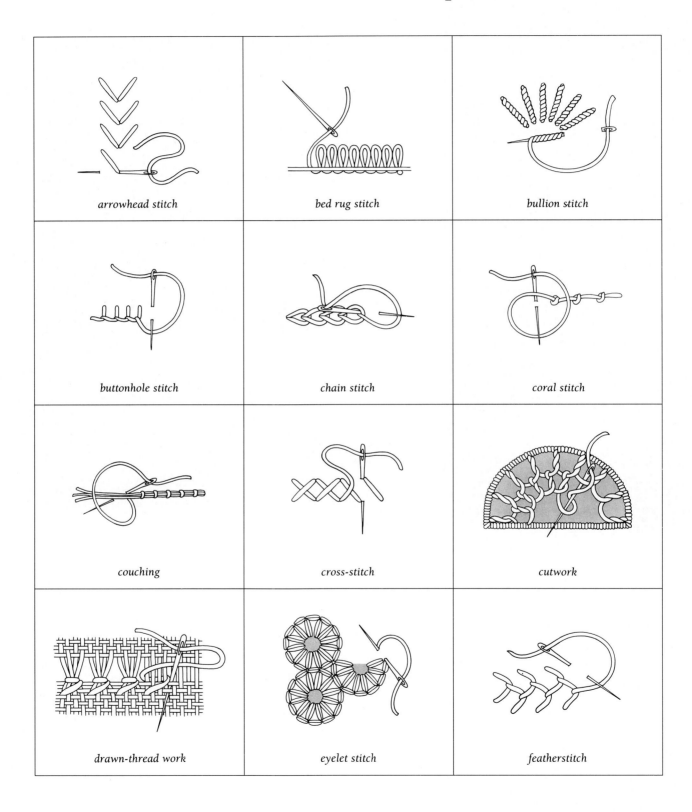

arrowhead stitch

bed rug stitch

bullion stitch

buttonhole stitch

chain stitch

coral stitch

couching

cross-stitch

cutwork

drawn-thread work

eyelet stitch

featherstitch

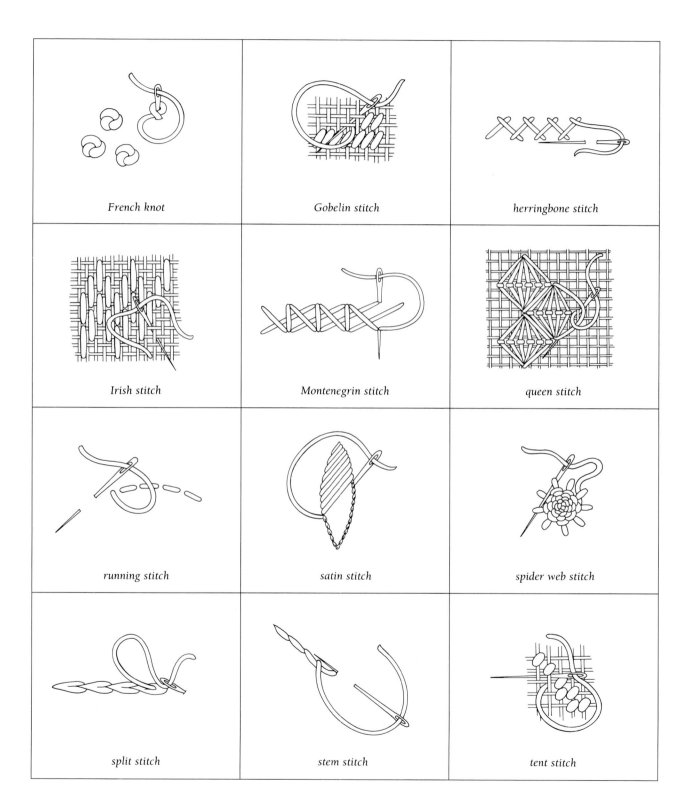

French knot	*Gobelin stitch*	*herringbone stitch*
Irish stitch	*Montenegrin stitch*	*queen stitch*
running stitch	*satin stitch*	*spider web stitch*
split stitch	*stem stitch*	*tent stitch*

Museum, Collection, and Photography Credits

Cover: needlework picture—Carol and Stephen Huber, East Lyme, CT; crewel blanket, Shaker pincushion, Victorian sewing pouch, wooden needlecase, beaded miser's purse, scrimshaw tape measure—collection of Rosalind and Edwin Miller; thimbles, scissors, silver filigree thimble case, silver walnut thimble case—Primrose Lane, Manhasset, NY; Hepplewhite chair and sewing table—Bernard and Dean Levy, Inc., NY/photo by Steven Mays. **Frontispiece**: The Metropolitan Museum of Art, NYC, gift of R. Thornton Wilson, 1943, in memory of Florence Ellsworth Wilson (43.16). **Page 8**: courtesy of the Henry Francis du Pont Winterthur Museum, Winterthur, DE. **Page 10**: courtesy of the Essex Institute, Salem, MA. **Page 11**: (top) photo by Paul Rocheleau; (bottom) reprinted by permission of Good Books, Intercourse, PA. **Page 12**: (top) Atwater Kent Museum, Philadelphia, PA; (bottom) courtesy of the Henry Francis du Pont Winterthur Museum, Winterthur, DE. **Page 13**: collection of Rosalind and Edwin Miller, courtesy of the Allentown Art Museum, Allentown, PA. **Page 14**: Shelburne Museum, Inc., Shelburne, VT/photo by Ken Burris. **Page 15**: The Metropolitan Museum of Art, NYC, bequest of Barbara Schiff Sinauer, 1984 (1984.331.3). **Page 16**: courtesy of the Henry Francis du Pont Winterthur Museum, Winterthur, DE. **Page 17**: Abby Aldrich Rockefeller Folk Art Center, Williamsburg, VA. **Page 18**: courtesy of the Essex Institute, Salem, MA. **Page 19**: courtesy of the Henry Francis du Pont Winterthur Museum, Winterthur, DE. **Pages 20-21**: (top row, left to right) New Haven Colony Historical Society, New Haven, CT; America Hurrah, NYC/photo by Rob Whitcomb; collection of Dr. and Mrs. Donald M. Herr/photo by Rob Whitcomb; collection of Dr. and Mrs. Donald M. Herr/photo by Rob Whitcomb; (middle row, left to right) courtesy of Stella Rubin/photo by Schecter Lee; collection of Rosemarie Machmer/photo courtesy of Thos. K. Woodard American Antiques & Quilts, NYC; courtesy of Stella

Rubin/photo by Schecter Lee; collection of Dr. and Mrs. Donald M. Herr/photo by Rob Whitcomb; (bottom row, left to right) collection of Dr. and Mrs. Donald M. Herr/photo by Rob Whitcomb; collection of Kathy Schoemer/photo courtesy of Thos. K. Woodard American Antiques & Quilts, NYC; collection of Kathy Schoemer/photo courtesy of Thos. K. Woodard American Antiques & Quilts, NYC; collection of Dr. and Mrs. Donald M. Herr/photo by Rob Whitcomb. **Page 22**: Museum of Art, Rhode Island School of Design, Providence, RI, gift of Mrs. Jesse H. Metcalf. **Page 23**: courtesy of Lyman Allyn Art Museum, New London, CT/photo by Steven Mays. **Page 24**: (top) courtesy of the Henry Francis du Pont Winterthur Museum, Winterthur, DE; (bottom) courtesy of the Museum of Fine Arts, Boston, Seth K. Sweetser Fund. **Page 25**: (top) collection of the Museum of American Folk Art, NYC, promised anonymous gift; (bottom) Colonial Williamsburg Foundation, Williamsburg, VA. **Page 26**: (left) The Metropolitan Museum of Art, NYC, gift of R. Thornton Wilson, 1943, in memory of Florence Ellsworth Wilson (43.16); (right top) courtesy of the Henry Francis du Pont Winterthur Museum, Winterthur, DE; (right bottom) America Hurrah, NYC. **Page 27**: (both) courtesy of the Henry Francis du Pont Winterthur Museum, Winterthur, DE. **Pages 28, 29**: (all) The Connecticut Historical Society, Hartford, CT. **Page 30**: Old Sturbridge Village, Sturbridge, MA/photo by Henry E. Peach. **Page 31**: Abby Aldrich Rockefeller Folk Art Center, Williamsburg, VA. **Page 32**: (top) Yale University Art Gallery, New Haven, CT, the Mabel Brady Garvan Collection; (bottom) Abby Aldrich Rockefeller Folk Art Center, Williamsburg, VA. **Page 33**: Abby Aldrich Rockefeller Folk Art Center, Williamsburg, VA. **Page 36**: (top) collection of the Albany Institute of History & Art, Albany, NY, bequest of Miss Louise Stafford Gilder; (bottom) collection of Rosalind and Edwin Miller, photo courtesy of the Allentown Museum, Allentown, PA. **Page 37**: (all)

Shelburne Museum, Inc., Shelburne, VT/photo by Ken Burris. **Page 38**: collection of Rosalind and Edwin Miller, photo courtesy of the Allentown Museum, Allentown, PA. **Page 39**: New Hampshire Historical Society, Concord, NH. **Page 40**: Schwenkfelder Library, Pennsburg, PA. **Page 41**: collection of Rosalind and Edwin Miller, photo courtesy of the Allentown Art Museum, Allentown, PA. **Pages 42-43**: collection of Rosalind and Edwin Miller/photo by Steven Mays. **Page 44**: collection of Rosalind and Edwin Miller, photo courtesy of the Allentown Art Museum, Allentown, PA. **Page 45**: The Metropolitan Museum of Art, NYC, purchase, 1980, funds from various donors (1980.63). **Pages 46, 47**: (all) collection of Rosalind and Edwin Miller/photos by Rob Whitcomb. **Page 48**: (top) collection of Rosalind and Edwin Miller/photo by Steven Mays; (bottom) courtesy of the Schenectady Museum and Planetarium, Schenectady, NY/photo by James N. Boorn. **Page 49**: (all) collection of Rosalind and Edwin Miller/photo by Steven Mays. **Page 50**: Shelburne Museum, Inc., Shelburne, VT/photo by Fred G. Hill. **Page 51**: (top row, left to right) collection of Rosalind and Edwin Miller/photo by Steven Mays; collection of Rosalind and Edwin Miller/photo by Steven Mays; courtesy of Evelyn Haertig/photo by Schecter Lee; (bottom row, left to right) courtesy of Evelyn Haertig/photo by Schecter Lee; collection of Rosalind and Edwin Miller/photo by Steven Mays; Shelburne Museum, Inc., Shelburne, VT/photo by Ken Burris. **Page 53**: (all) courtesy of the Henry Francis du Pont Winterthur Museum, Winterthur, DE. **Page 54**: (top row, left to right) courtesy of Stella Rubin/photo by Schecter Lee; Philadelphia Museum of Art, Philadelphia, PA, gift of Dr. John Joseph Stoudt; Shelburne Museum, Inc., Shelburne, VT/photo by Ken Burris; (middle row, left to right) courtesy of Jeannine Dobbs/photo by Schecter Lee; Shelburne Museum, Inc., Shelburne, VT/photo by Ken Burris; collection of Rosalind and Edwin Miller/photo by Steven Mays; (bottom row, left to right) reprinted by permission of Good Books, Intercourse, PA; courtesy of David Pottinger; reprinted by permission of Good Books, Intercourse, PA. **Page 55**: (top row, all) courtesy of Stella Rubin/photo by Schecter Lee; (bottom row, left to right) reprinted by permission of Good Books, Intercourse, PA; courtesy of David Pottinger; courtesy of David Pottinger. **Page 56**: collection of the Museum of American Folk Art, NYC, gift of the Trustees of the Museum of American Folk Art (1979.7.1). **Page 58**: courtesy of the Wenham Historical Association and Museum, Inc., Wenham, MA. **Page 59**: Yale University Art Gallery, New Haven, CT, the Mabel Brady Garvan Collection. **Page 60**: courtesy of the Art Institute of Chicago, Chicago, IL, gift of the Needlework and Textile Guild of Chicago (1944.27). **Page 61**: from the collections of Henry Ford Museum & Greenfield Village, Dearborn, MI (24-B-145). **Pages 62, 63**: Shelburne Museum, Inc., Shelburne, VT/photos by Ken Burris. **Pages 64-65**: courtesy of Cora Ginsburg, Inc., NYC/photo by Steven Mays. **Pages 66, 67**: (all) Old York Historical Society, York, Maine. **Page 68**: from the collections of Henry Ford Museum & Greenfield Village, Dearborn, MI (24-B-50). **Page 69**: Colonial Williamsburg Foundation, Williamsburg, VA. **Page 70**: America Hurrah, NYC. **Page 71**: courtesy of Kelter-Malcé, NYC/photo by Schecter Lee. **Pages 72, 73**: America Hurrah, NYC. **Pages 74-75**: sewing boxes, leather needlebook, tartanware drum case, Mauchline wooden cases (on sewing box), Mauchline wooden bottle case, burled acorn case, brass thimbles, stone needle pusher—Tender Buttons, NYC; horseshoe case, silver walnut case, folk-art rabbit case, plastic cases, star case and gold thimble, thimble rings, glass thimbles, cloisonné thimbles, advertising thimbles, leather thimble, silver thimbles, delft thimble—Primose Lane, Manhasset, ·NY/photo by Stephen Donelian. **Pages 76-82**: (all) Shelburne Museum, Inc., Shelburne, VT/photos by Ken Burris. **Page 83**: collection of the Museum of American Folk

Art, NYC, gift of the Trustees of the Museum of American Folk Art (1979.7.1). **Page 84**: America Hurrah, NYC. **Page 85**: Thos. K. Woodard American Antiques & Quilts, NYC. **Page 86**: Shelburne Museum, Inc., Shelburne, VT/photo by Ken Burris. **Page 87**: © Chun Y. Lai/Esto. **Page 88**: Shelburne Museum, Inc., Shelburne, VT/photo by Ken Burris. **Page 89**: America Hurrah, NYC/photo by Steven Mays. **Pages 90-91**: (background quilt) America Hurrah, NYC; (top row, left to right) collection of Sandra Mitchell; Robert Cargo Folk Art Gallery, Tuscaloosa, AL; America Hurrah, NYC; (bottom row, left) America Hurrah, NYC; (bottom row, right) The Quilt Digest Press, San Francisco, CA, first published in *The Quilt Digest 2*. **Page 92**: Shelburne Museum, Inc., Shelburne, VT/photo by Ken Burris. **Page 94**: courtesy of the Pilgrim Society, Plymouth, MA. **Page 95**: (top) courtesy of the Henry Francis du Pont Winterthur Museum, Winterthur, DE; (bottom) the Allentown Art Museum, Allentown, PA, gift of the Reverend and Mrs. Van S. Merle-Smith, Jr. **Page 96**: (top) collection of Frank and Barbara Pollack; (bottom) courtesy of Harold and Judith Weissman/photo by Schecter Lee. **Page 97**: Shelburne Museum, Inc., Shelburne, VT/photo by Ken Burris. **Page 98**: (top) Shelburne Museum, Inc., Shelburne, VT; (bottom) America Hurrah, NYC. **Page 99**: (top) courtesy of Jeannine Dobbs/photo by Schecter Lee; (bottom) collection of Gail van der Hoof and Jonathan Holstein/photo courtesy of Thos. K. Woodard American Antiques & Quilts, NYC. **Page 100**: Seaver Center for Western History Research, Natural History Museum of Los Angeles County, Los Angeles, CA. **Page 101**: (top) Eleanor and Stephen Score/photo courtesy of Thos. K. Woodard American Antiques & Quilts, NYC; (bottom) Thos. K. Woodard American Antiques & Quilts, NYC. **Pages 102, 103**: (all) collection of Rosalind and Edwin Miller/photo by Steven Mays. **Pages 104, 105**: (all) Pocumtuck Valley Memorial Association, Memorial Hall Museum, Deerfield, MA.

Page 106: America Hurrah, NYC. **Page 108**: private collection. **Page 109**: (both) America Hurrah, NYC. **Page 110**: (top) collection of Courcier and Wilkins, photo courtesy of America Hurrah, NYC; (bottom) New York State Historical Association, Cooperstown, NY. **Page 111**: (top) Old Sturbridge Village, Sturbridge, MA/photo by Henry E. Peach; (bottom) Shelburne Museum, Inc., Shelburne, VT/photo by Ken Burris. **Page 112**: (both) private collection. **Page 114**: America Hurrah, NYC. **Page 115**: Shelburne Museum, Inc., Shelburne, VT/photo by Ken Burris. **Page 116**: (top) collection of Barbara Johnson; (bottom) America Hurrah, NYC. **Page 117**: (both) America Hurrah, NYC. **Page 118**: (both) America Hurrah, NYC. **Page 119**: (top) Shaker Village of Pleasant Hill, Harrodsburg, KY; (bottom) America Hurrah, NYC. **Page 120**: (top) America Hurrah, NYC; (bottom) courtesy of David A. Schorsch, Inc., NYC. **Pages 121-124**: (all) collection of Barbara Johnson. **Page 125**: (top) collection of Barbara Johnson; (bottom) Shelburne Museum, Inc., Shelburne, VT/photo by Ken Burris. **Page 126**: (both) © Esto. **Page 127**: (top) America Hurrah, NYC; (bottom) collection of Barbara Johnson/photo by Schecter Lee. **Page 128**: (both) collection of Barbara Johnson. **Page 129**: (top) America Hurrah, NYC; (bottom) collection of Dr. and Mrs. Donald M. Herr/photo © 1977 by Anita Schorsch, from her book *Pastoral Dreams* published by Main Street Press, Universe Books. **Page 130**: (left) America Hurrah, NYC; (right) collection of Barbara Johnson. **Page 131**: (top) collection of Barbara Johnson; (bottom) America Hurrah, NYC. **Page 132**: from the collections of Henry Ford Museum & Greenfield Village, Dearborn, MI (24-G-213). **Page 133**: (top) collection of Rosalind and Edwin Miller; (bottom) The Metropolitan Museum of Art, NYC, Sansbury-Mills Fund, 1961 (61.47.1). **Pages 134-135**: (portrait) from the collections of Henry Ford Museum & Greenfield Village, Dearborn, MI (B42301); (top row, left, and bottom row, left) from the *Descriptive Catalogue of E. S. Frost & Co.'s Hooked Rug Patterns,* © 1970 by The Edison Institute, Dearborn, MI; (top row, right, and second row, both) from the collections of Henry Ford Museum & Greenfield Village, Dearborn, MI (D8004); (third row, left) courtesy of The Winterthur Library, Printed Book and Periodical Collection, Winterthur, DE; (third row, right) private collection/photo by Bradley Olman; (bottom row, right) collection of Barbara Johnson. **Page 136:** (top) private collection; (bottom) private collection/photo by George Ross. **Page 137:** collection of Susan and Richard Berman/photo by Steven Mays. **Page 138:** (top) Shelburne Museum, Inc., Shelburne, VT/photo by Ken Burris; (bottom) © Chun Y. Lai/Esto. **Page 139:** Shelburne Museum, Inc., Shelburne, VT/photo by Ken Burris. **Page 140:** photo by Paul Rocheleau. **Page 141:** (top) courtesy of Kelter-Malcé, NYC/photo by Schecter Lee; (bottom) reprinted by permission of Good Books, Intercourse, PA. **Pages 142, 143:** The Metropolitan Museum of Art, NYC, gift of Katherine Keyes, in memory of her father, Homer Eaton Keyes, 1938 (38.157). **Pages 144-153:** textile and needlework collection of June and Alan Goodrich, Antiques-Folk Art, Erwinna, PA/photos by George Ross. **Pages 154-157:** needlework collection of Carol and Stephen Huber, East Lyme, CT/photos by George Ross. **Pages 158-165:** needlework collection of Thos. K. Woodard American Antiques & Quilts, NYC/photos by George Ross. **Pages 166, 167:** illustrations by Ray Skibinski.

Index

Acknowledgments

Our thanks to Linda Baumgarten of the Colonial Williamsburg Foundation, Susan and Richard Berman, Alberta Brandt of the Henry Francis du Pont Winterthur Museum, Kathy Francis of the Museum of American Textile History, Riki Gail, Cora Ginsburg, Merle Good of Good Books, June and Alan Goodrich, Blanche Greenstein, Catherine H. Grosfils of the Colonial Williamsburg Foundation, Titi Halle, Dr. and Mrs. Donald M. Herr, Carol and Stephen Huber, Susan and Stephen Hunkins, Barbara Johnson, Kate and Joel Kopp, Rosalind and Edwin Miller, Celia Oliver of Shelburne Museum, Inc., David Pottinger, Robert Shaw of Shelburne Museum, Inc., Laurie Suber of the Colonial Williamsburg Foundation, Susan Swan of the Henry Francis du Pont Winterthur Museum, Anne Watkins of the Abby Aldrich Rockefeller Folk Art Center, and Thomas K. Woodard for their help on this book.

First printing
Published simultaneously in Canada
School and library distribution by Silver Burdett Company,
Morristown, New Jersey

TIME-LIFE is a trademark of Time Incorporated U.S.A.

Production by Giga Communications, Inc.
Printed in U.S.A.

Library of Congress Cataloging-in-Publication Data

The Needle arts
p.   cm. — (American country)
Includes index.
ISBN 0-8094-6841-7 — ISBN 0-8094-6842-5 (lib. bdg.)
1. Needlework—United States.
2. Decorative arts, Early American.
I. Time-Life Books.   II. Series.
NK8803.5.N44   1990   746'.0974—dc20   90-11002
CIP

American Country was created by Rebus, Inc., and published by Time-Life Books.

REBUS, INC.

Publisher: RODNEY FRIEDMAN • Editor: MARYA DALRYMPLE
Executive Editor: RACHEL D. CARLEY • Managing Editor: BRENDA SAVARD • Consulting Editor: CHARLES L. MEE, JR.
Copy Editor: ALEXA RIPLEY BARRE
Writers: JUDITH CRESSY, ROSEMARY G. RENNICKE • Freelance Writer: JOE L. ROSSON
Design Editors: NANCY MERNIT, CATHRYN SCHWING
Test Kitchen Director: GRACE YOUNG • Editor, The Country Letter: BONNIE J. SLOTNICK
Contributing Editors: LEE CUTRONE, ANNE MOFFAT, CATHERINE RITZINGER
Indexer: MARILYN FLAIG

Art Director: JUDITH HENRY • Associate Art Director: SARA REYNOLDS
Designers: AMY BERNIKER, TIMOTHY JEFFS
Photographer: STEVEN MAYS • Photo Editor: SUE ISRAEL
Photo Assistant: ROB WHITCOMB • Freelance Photographers: STEPHEN DONELIAN, GEORGE ROSS
Freelance Photo Stylists: VALORIE FISHER, DEE SHAPIRO • Set Carpenter: MARCOS SORENSEN

Special Consultant for this book: MARGARET VINCENT
Series Consultants: BOB CAHN, HELAINE W. FENDELMAN, LINDA C. FRANKLIN, GLORIA GALE,
KATHLEEN EAGEN JOHNSON, JUNE SPRIGG, CLAIRE WHITCOMB

Time-Life Books Inc. is a wholly owned subsidiary of THE TIME INC. BOOK COMPANY.

President and Chief Executive Officer: KELSO F. SUTTON
President, Time Inc. Books Direct: CHRISTOPHER T. LINEN

TIME-LIFE BOOKS INC.

Editor: GEORGE CONSTABLE
Director of Design: LOUIS KLEIN • Director of Editorial Resources: PHYLLIS K. WISE
Director of Photography and Research: JOHN CONRAD WEISER

President: JOHN M. FAHEY JR.
Senior Vice Presidents: ROBERT M. DeSENA, PAUL R. STEWART, CURTIS G. VIEBRANZ, JOSEPH J. WARD
Vice Presidents: STEPHEN L. BAIR, BONITA L. BOEZEMAN, MARY P. DONOHOE, STEPHEN L. GOLDSTEIN,
ANDREW P. KAPLAN, TREVOR LUNN, SUSAN J. MARUYAMA, ROBERT H. SMITH
New Product Development: TREVOR LUNN, DONIA ANN STEELE
Supervisor of Quality Control: JAMES KING

Publisher: JOSEPH J. WARD

For information about any Time-Life book please call 1-800-621-7026, or write:
Reader Information, Time-Life Customer Service
P.O. Box C-32068, Richmond, Virginia 23261-2068

Time-Life Books Inc. offers a wide range of fine recordings, including a Rock 'n' Roll Era series.
For subscription information, call 1-800-621-7026, or write TIME-LIFE MUSIC,
P.O. Box C-32068, Richmond, Virginia 23261-2068.